Doctrinal Interpretation of Law

This dissertation was approved by the Very Rev. John Rogg Schmidt, J.C.D., Associate Professor of Canon Law, as director, and by the Rev. Romaeus O'Brien, O.Carm., J.C.D., and the Rt. Rev. Clement Bastnagel, J.C.D., as readers.

THE CATHOLIC UNIVERSITY OF AMERICA
CANON LAW STUDIES
No. 345

Doctrinal Interpretation of Law
A Historical Synopsis and a Commentary

A DISSERTATION

Submitted to the Faculty of the School of Canon Law of The Catholic University of America in Partial Fulfillment of the Requirements for the Degree of Doctor of Canon Law

BY

REVEREND MATTHEW M. SHEKLETON, O.S.M., J.C.L.
Priest of the American Province of the Servite Fathers

THE CATHOLIC UNIVERSITY OF AMERICA PRESS
WASHINGTON, D. C.
1961

Imprimi Potest:
VERY REV. LOUIS CORTNEY, O.S.M.
Prior Provincial

Chicago Illinois, November 2, 1960

Nihil Obstat:
RT. REV. CLEMENT BASTNAGEL, J.C.D.
Censor Deputatus

Washington, D. C., November 14, 1960

Imprimatur:
ALBERT CARDINAL MEYER, S.T.D., S.S.L.
Archbishop of Chicago

Chicago, Illinois, November 10, 1960

Printed by
THE WICKERSHAM PRINTING COMPANY
Lancaster, Pennsylvania

FOREWORD

There are two aspects to be considered in every branch of human learning; the consideration of the principles, and the application of those principles to concrete situations. The consideration of the principles concerns the *science,* and the application of these to the concrete concerns the *art.* For science is concerned with knowing and art with doing.[1]

There are also two aspects to legal interpretation. One concerns the pure, ideal interpretation consisting in principles. Its purpose is to examine and explain the rules for the proper understanding of laws. It is concerned with the theory of interpretation, and this is called the *science* of interpretation.

The other aspect considers these principles as applied to particular and concrete cases, with due advertence to all the individual circumstances of person, time, place, etc. Its purpose is to discover the meaning of this particular law, to solve this particular doubt, to reconcile this particular contradiction. It applies the rules or the principles of interpretation, and this is called the *art* of interpretation.

Thus the science of interpretation exists only that it may be applied. It would have no purpose if there were not individual laws to interpret. On the other hand, the art of interpretation could not exist unless there were principles to direct it. It concerns itself with practice, but in so doing it recognizes and applies the theory. For no practice is reasonable except insofar as it is based upon sound theory.

Accordingly, actual interpretation of law presupposes both the science and the art of interpretation. It presupposes the art, because without individual laws there can be no interpretation. It presupposes the science, for without true guiding principles there can be no true understanding of law.

Though there is a close connection between the science and the art of interpretation, and though the actual interpretation of

[1] Cf. Aristotle, lib. VI *Ethicorum,* cap. III and IV.

law postulates both, a discussion of the science does not necessarily involve a discussion of the art. The principle or theory can indeed be considered apart from all advertence to a particular concrete application of the principle or theory.

The present study concerns itself with a discussion of the *science* of interpretation, that is, an exposition of the theory and general principles of interpretation, and makes no pretense to any treating of the art of interpretation.

With the science of interpretation, therefore, as the material object, the formal object will be limited to a study of *doctrinal* interpretation, for it is in this field that the science of interpretation most properly belongs. The principles of this aspect of scientific interpretation are set forth by the ecclesiastical legislator in canon 18. This study, therefore, concerns itself in a large part with an examination and exposition of that canon.

In order that this subject be treated more completely, there has been included a short history of interpretation from Roman times to the period just preceding the Code.

Sincere gratitude is humbly expressed to the Superiors whose love for scholarship and spirit of sacrifice have made possible for the writer this opportunity for special study; to the members of the Faculty of the School of Canon Law for their patience and kind assistance; and to all who have been of help and encouragement in the preparation of this study.

TABLE OF CONTENTS

PAGE

PART II
CANONICAL COMMENTARY

CHAPTER V

CHAPTER VI

CHAPTER VII

CHAPTER VIII

PART I

HISTORICAL SYNOPSIS

CHAPTER I

DOCTRINAL INTERPRETATION IN ROMAN LAW

"Law shall be clearly expressed, lest by its obscurity it lead to misunderstanding," said Gratian.[1] However, it is impossible to obtain this in every instance; hence it is necessary to interpret law, lest its force be frustrated in practice.

Interpretation, in the modern sense of the term, may be defined as the act of finding out the true sense of any form of words—that is, the sense which the author intended to convey—and of enabling others to derive from them the same idea which the author intended to convey.[2]

Interpretation had an important rôle in the development of Roman Law. However, it would be incorrect to try to force any historical account of a juridic institute into a modern mould, that is, to attempt to fit an ancient system into modern concepts. Therefore, though one may attempt to trace the history of the modern concept of doctrinal interpretation from Roman Law to the present, it would be misleading to create the impression that Roman Law had a definite and uniform system of doctrinal interpretation. Hence it is necessary to give a brief exposition of *"interpretatio"* in Roman Law, and then to attempt to show how doctrinal interpretation fits into this picture.

The first certain landmark in the history of Roman Law is the *Law of the Twelve Tables*. There are indeed traditions of legislation by more or less legendary kings, who established a collection of *"leges regiae"* which were of a sacred character and belonged to the borderland between law and religion. But these play no important part in later law.[3] The *Law of the XII Tables*

[1] C. 2, D. IV. "Erit autem lex . . . manifesta ne aliquid per obscuritatem in captionem contineat. . . ."

[2] Walter A. Shumaker and George Foster Longsdorf, *The Cyclopedic Law Dictionary* (2. ed., by James C. Cahill, Chicago: Callagahan and Company, 1922), p. 546.

[3] Buckland, *A Text-Book of Roman Law from Augustus to Justinian* (2. ed., Cambridge University Press, 1932), p. 1.

was looked upon by later Romans as the starting point of their legal history. Livy (59 B.C.–17 A.D.) called them "the fountain of all public and private law."[4] But the *XII Tables* did not contain the whole law; they simply stated general principles, the interpretation of which was left to a college of officials called *"pontifices."*[5] To that period may be referred the interpretation of law by legal fictions, that is, contrivances by which a legal rule or institution was diverted from its original purpose to accomplish some other object.[6] As one understands the meaning of the term today, this could scarcely be called interpretation, except in the very widest sense of the word. However, such was the authority of the *pontifices* that one may conclude that their interpretation was "authentic" in the modern sense of the word.[7]

The ascendancy of the pontiffs came to an end in the fourth century B.C., and the task of interpretation passed into the hands of the jurists (*"iuris consulti"* or *"iuris prudentes"*). They were the real builders of the great fabric of Roman Law.[8] The jurists in the time of the Republic engaged in activities which are described in semitechnical language as *respondere, cavere, scribere* and *agere*. They advised clients, or the magistrates, or the judges (*respondere*). They saw that legal forms were properly employed and they drafted legal documents (*cavere—scribere*). They undertook the general conduct of litigation (*agere*). They gave their *"responsa"* to the advocates and the judges if they were in doubt. These were in no way binding on the judges, but owed their weight to the personal reputation of the jurist. However the judges seldom failed to follow their advice, and in this manner they exercised a great influence on law.[9] Can not one say

[4] Livy, Book 3, Chap. 34.

[5] Digest (1. 2) (2. 6).

[6] R. W. Lee, *Elements of Roman Law* (London, 1944), p. 8.

[7] Schmidt, *The Principles of Authentic Interpretation in Canon 17 of the Code of Canon Law,* The Catholic University of America Canon Law Studies, n. 141 (Washington, D.C.: The Catholic University of America Press, 1941), pp. 13-14.

[8] Buckland, *op. cit.,* p. 20.

[9] Jolowicz, *Historical Introduction to the Study of Roman Law* (London, 1932) pp. 92-93.

therefore that the jurists of that time gave what might roughly correspond to our idea of doctrinal interpretation of law?

Regarding their method of interpretation, it can be stated that sometimes it was based on the letter of the statute, and that sometimes it was freer, so that the practical needs and matters of policy, and not the letter of the law, determined the interpretation.[10] Two classical examples show how this type of interpretation helped to develop Roman Law. According to the *XII Tables,* if a father sold his son into slavery three times, he lost his paternal power (aimed at checking the cruelty and avarice of some fathers). By interpretation this type of transaction was employed to emancipate the son. This is certainly a departure from the original meaning of the law.[11] Again, according to the *Lex Voconia* a testator of the wealthiest class could not name a woman as his heir in his will. By interpretation the right of females to succeed in intestate succession was restricted.[12]

When the Republic gave way to the Empire, certain jurists were given the *ius publice respondendi,* that is, the right of giving certain responses authorized by the emperor.[13] By the time of Gaius (2nd century) these jurists had attained such high authority that he enumerated them among the sources of written law and described them as rendering "the decisions and opinions of persons authorized to lay down the law" (*sententiae et opiniones eorum quibus permissum est iura condere*).[14] Still no juristic text suggests that Augustus (27 B.C.–14 A.D.) actually made these *responsa* binding. Perhaps Augustus did not change the legal position of the *responsa,* but a license from the em-

[10] D. (1. 2) (2. 12), Pomponius: "Ita in civitate nostra aut iure, id est lege, (XII Tabulae, iuxta Glossam) constituitur, aut est proprium ius civile, quod sine scripto in sola prudentium interpretatione consistit."

[11] XII Tab. (4, 2); Gaius (1, 132); Buckland, *op. cit.,* pp. 121-122.

[12] Sententiae Pauli (4, 8) 20: "Feminae ad hereditates legitimas ultra consanguineas successiones non admittuntur: idque iure civili Voconiana ratione videtur effectum. Ceterum lex XII Tabularum nulla discretione sexus cognatos admittit."

[13] Inst. (1. 2) 8.

[14] Gaius (1, 7).

peror could not fail before long to give these privileged *responsa* an overriding influence on the mind of the judge.[15]

The change from pre-classical times which was most striking however was the technique employed in expanding the law. The use of simulated transactions and procedural rules practically disappeared. Classical jurisprudence freed itself from the limitations inherent in that type of interpretation. It became the practice to base *responsa* upon the reason of the law (*ratio legis*). This afforded a simple means of expanding the sphere of application of rules established for a particular situation. Simply stated, from a given rule of law a major premise was established; as a logical consequence a series of other rules was derived, not directly contained within the source from which the premise was derived.[16] Occasional instances of *"per consequentias," "ad exemplum,"* and the like are indicative of interpretation by analogy.[17] Cases which the law omitted but which fell within its principles were analogous to cases which fell within its principle and which it actually included.[18] In addition thereto its sphere was enlarged to include the *"argumentum a contrario"* [19] the *"argumentum a maiori ad minus"* [20] and the *"argumentum a fortiori."* [21]

However in classical times there also developed the idea of attempting to determine the actual intent of the legislator when

[15] Buckland, *op. cit.,* p. 24.

[16] R. Sohm, *The Institutes. A Textbook of the History and System of Roman Private Law,* 3. ed. translated by J. C. Ledlie, Oxford: Clarendon Press, 1926, pp. 31-33.

[17] Cuq, *Manuel des Institutions Juridiques des Romains* (2 vols., Paris, 1891-1902) p. 44, n. 7.

[18] Ulpian in D. (1. 3) 13: For as Pedius says, whenever this or that is provided by statute, there is good opportunity for other rules, when they involve the same beneficial principle, to be supplied either by *"interpretatio"* or by *magisterial ruling.* Cf. also D. (1. 3) 12: "Extend the rule to analogous cases," and D. (1. 3) 27: "It is the essence of a statute that it should be applicable to any persons or things which may at any time be similar to those specified."

[19] D. (22. 5) 18 and D. (28. 1) (20. 6) *lex Julia de adulteriis.*

[20] D. (50. 17) 21.

[21] D. (50. 17) 26.

it was inadequately expressed. Whereas the older art of the pontiffs and of the early jurists paid little attention to the meaning of the words of the statutes, the newer interpretation concerned itself with a search for the meaning of the words, particularly with regard to the sense in which they were used by the legislator.[22] This may be called grammatical interpretation. Such grammatical interpretation is evidenced by the juristic literature of the second and early first century B.C.[23]

Alongside this grammatical interpretation there is to be found what is now termed logical interpretation. This system sought to interpret the meaning of the law from the intention of the lawgiver rather than from its wording. The co-existence of the two views is reflected in the conflict between the word (*verbum, scriptum*) and the intention (*voluntas, sententia*).[24]

The Roman rhetors had a very well developed system of interpretation which can readily be seen in some excerpts from the writings of Cicero (106-43 B.C.). In his *De Inventione* he wrote:

> Every subject which contains in itself any controversy existing in language or in disputation, contains a question either of fact, or of name, or of a class, or of an action. This question from which a cause arises we call *"constitutio."*[25] . . . In the next place it is to be considered whether the controversy depends upon reasoning or upon writing. For a controversy upon writing is one which arises out of the nature of the writing. And of that there are five types which have been separated from statements of causes. Firstly when the words themselves seem to depart from the intention of the writer; then when two or more laws are discrepant among themselves; then when that which has been written signifies two or more things; then from that which has been written something is discovered which was not written; finally, when the effect of the words is inquired into, as if it were a question of definition (in the statement

[22] Cuq, *op. cit.*, p. 43.

[23] Cf. the writings of Aelius Stilo († 74 B.C.), Marcus Varro († 27 B.C.) and Aelius Gallus (1st Cent.)

[24] A. Arthur Schiller, "Roman Interpretatio and Anglo American Interpretation and Construction," *The Virginia Law Review*, Vol. 27, April 1941, pp. 749-750.

[25] *De Inventione*, 1. 8. 10.

> of a case), in which it has been noted. Wherefore the first type we call writing versus intention, the second contradictory laws, the third ambiguity, the fourth consequential, the fifth definition.[26]

Later in the same work, having disposed of the controversies depending upon reasoning, that is disputes as to matters of fact, Cicero returned to disputes upon writing and told what was to be done in each of the five cases noted. The typical sorts of arguments that could be used by the rhetors were illustrated with some fragments from his advice regarding argumentation in the case of ambiguity.

> First if it can be done, it ought to be shown that the writing is not ambiguous because persons are wont to use that one word or more in ordinary speech in the meaning in which the speaker will show it is here to be understood. Then it ought to be shown that what is sought is made clear from preceding and subsequent language, whereas if the words were considered by themselves, all or most of them would be ambiguous. Then, it is necessary to understand what the writer had in mind, from his other writings and acts, speeches, disposition and his normal life, and examine that document itself in which the ambiguity occurs, which is the subject of the dispute, throughout all its parts, to see whether there is anything opposing that interpretation of ours contrary to that which the opponent insists upon.[27]

From these few Ciceronian fragments one can readily see the high degree of skill attained by the rhetors in their development of interpretation. However, there is a dispute among authors regarding the prevalence of this system among the jurists.

In the late Empire the line of jurists ceased somewhat suddenly, perhaps because of the increasing absolutism of the Emperor, who no longer gave the *"ius respondendi"* but exercised his own interpretation of the law.[28] However, the great importance of the classical jurists was recognized by the emperors, who continued to look upon them as authorities and guides in the interpretation of law. Thus Constantine, in the year 321,

[26] *De Inventione,* 13. 17.

[27] *De Inventione,* 2. 40. 116-117.

[28] Buckland, *op. cit.,* p. 32.

enacted that certain notes of Ulpianus († 228) and Paulus († cir. 231) on Papinianus († 212) were not to be of authority, a sign that the great jurists had actually acquired authority.[29]

Theodosius II (408-450) enacted the Law of Citations in 426 in which the works of Papinianus, Paulus, Gaius, Ulpianus and Modestinus (middle of 3rd century) were constituted the primary authorities. When there was a difference of opinion, the majority was to be followed, if there was no majority opinion, then Papinianus. If he was silent, then the judge could rely on his own discreet option.[30]

A century later Justinian (527-565) directed the compilers of the *Digest* not to select any view simply because it had a majority in its favor, since opinions were to be estimated by weight, not by number.[31]

However Justinian insisted on a general imperial power of interpretation, and forbade all commentaries on the *Digest,* whence doctrinal interpretation could have sprung. Doubts of law and obscurities in the law were to be referred to the Emperor for solution.[32]

From the foregoing one may conclude that a substantial foundation of doctrinal interpretation was built by the Roman jurists. Later on in the tracing of the history of doctrinal interpretation in Canon Law, one will note how the canonists were able to incorporate many of these legal principles into Canon Law.

[29] C. Th. (1. 4) 1.

[30] C. Th. (1. 4) 3.

[31] Buckland, *op. cit.,* p. 34.

[32] C. (1. 14) 9.

CHAPTER II

INFLUENCE OF THE FATHERS OF THE CHURCH ON THE DEVELOPMENT AND INTERPRETATION OF LAW

ARTICLE I. THE FATHERS OF THE FIRST THREE CENTURIES

In the first three centuries of the Church's history there was very little written Ecclesiastical Law. It was not necessary, for the faithful lived mainly according to the divine and apostolic traditions handed down from generation to generation. However, it would not be correct to say that there was no ecclesiastical law in those days. Christ Himself established the fundamental constitution of the Church and enacted not only moral and dogmatic but also juridical precepts, which were supplemented by the Apostles in virtue of the power given to them by Christ.[1]

The traits of the early ecclesiastical law have been preserved for us in the works of the Fathers and Ecclesiastical writers. But the Fathers of the first three centuries did more than merely preserve the law, for they helped to define it by interpreting and supplementing the rules given by Christ and His apostles. The teaching put forth in their writings played a considerable part in the very formation of law itself.[2] There was no real science of Canon Law at that time, nor was there to be for centuries to come. Yet the Fathers in their writings on moral and dogmatic subjects had incidentally much to say on that

[1] See authors who have written on public ecclesiastical law, e.g., Ottaviani, *Institutiones Iuris Publici Ecclesiastici* (2. ed., 2 vols., Typis Polyglottis Vaticanis, 1935-1936), I, *Ius Publicum* Internum (*Ecclesiae Constitutio Socialis et Potestas*), pp. 233-244.

[2] Le Bras, "La doctrine, source des collections canoniques," *Recueil d'Etudes sur les Sources du Droit en l'Honneur de François Gény* (3 vols., Paris: Recueil Sirey, 1934), I, 69-76.

which was purely disciplinary.[3] They were not only the preachers of the Faith, the guardians and witnesses of Tradition, the interpreters of Scripture and the teachers of Morals, but also the *"canonum-magistri atque iurium Ecclesiae defensores."*[4] When the fundamental rules of Church law began to be expressed in written canons, the ancient traditions, explained and carried on in the works of the early Fathers, did not lose their force.[5]

ARTICLE II. THE FATHERS FROM THE FOURTH CENTURY

The religious peace which came to the Church after the persecutions, and the legal status given to the Church by the Roman Empire, enabled it to function more freely. Written law gradually began to replace custom and tradition. The exercise of the authority of the Supreme Pontiff became more evident with the issuance of decretal letters, and Church Councils both ecumenical and particular became more frequent.[6] However, this did not mean that the Fathers no longer exercised any influence on the development of ecclesiastical law. The fact is that a great part of the legislation put forth by the councils both local and ecumenical was ignored. The councils of the East were for the most part local councils, and even the list of ecumenical councils was not settled without considerable difficulty; the councils of Africa and Europe were directed toward specific regions and the papal decretals to specified recipients.[7] The increased output therefore of conciliar canons and papal decretals did not have the desired effect of bringing about a unification of discipline. Meanwhile in the absence of a universally recognized discipline it was natural that the opinions of the Fathers should continue

[3] Zallinger, *Institutionum Juris Ecclesiastici Publici et Privati Liber Subsidiarius I* (Romae, 1823), pp. 133-134.

[4] Zallinger, *loc. cit.;* Wernz, *Ius Decretalium* (6 vols., Romae-Prati, 1898-1914), I, n. 186.

[5] Wernz, *Ius Decretalium,* I, n. 185.

[6] Van Hove, *Commentarium Lovaniense in Codicem Iuris Canonici,* Vol. I, tom. I, *Prolegomena ad Codicem Iuris Canonici* (2. ed., Mechliniae-Romae: H. Dessain, 1945), pp. 136-140 (hereafter cited *Prolegomena*).

[7] Van Hove, *Prolegomena,* pp. 143-149.

to have considerable influence on the practice and growth of law.[8] Already in the fourth century and more so in the fifth, the popes and the councils began to appeal to the works of the earlier writers for testimony in support of their own opinions.[9]

At the same time, however, it was realized that not all of the Fathers could be appealed to as reliable witnesses, since some had fallen into error. In the fifth century, efforts were made to set up a criterion by which to discriminate between those whose testimony was reliable and those whose testimony could not be depended upon. The criterion and the conditions on which their testimony was to be accepted were clearly stated by Vincent of Lerins († cir. 445) in his *Commonitoria,* composed about the year 434.[10] In the fifth century therefore the agreement among the Fathers furnished one of the strongest arguments for the truth of a doctrine.[11] Yet this agreement among the Fathers was not to be the ordinary rule of faith. This was the living Magisterium of the Church, and only when the Church had made no decision were they to be appealed to.[12] So it is a fact beyond doubt that the Fathers had come to have a very definitely recognized authority.

Because of this growing respect and authority given to their writings, the texts of the Fathers were given a large and increas-

[8] For example, on re-baptism and re-ordination, see Saltet, *Les Réordinations: Etude sur le Sacrement de l'Ordre,* (2. ed., Paris, 1907) pp. 1-83; Waldron, *The Minister of Baptism,* The Catholic University of America Canon Law Studies, n. 170 (Washington, D.C.: The Catholic University of America Press, 1942), pp. 16-17.

[9] For numerous references see Chapman, "Fathers of the Church," *The Catholic Encyclopedia: An International Work of Reference on the Constitution, Doctrine, Discipline and History of the Catholic Church* (edited by Charles J. Herbermann, Edward A. Pace, Conde B. Pallen, Thomas J. Shahan, John J. Wynne, assisted by numerous collaborators, 15 vols., Index, and Supplement, New York, 1907-1922), VI, 1-18 (cf. pp. 2-4).

[10] *Florilegium Patristicum,* Fasc. V: *Vincentii Lerinensis Commonitoria* (digessit, vertit, adnotavit Gerhardus Rauschen, Bonnae, 1906) (hereafter cited as *Commonitoria*).

[11] *Commonitoria,* cap. XXVIII—*ibid.,* pp. 59-62.

[12] *Commonitoria,* capp. III, XXVII, XXVIII, XXIX—*ibid.,* pp. 12-13, 58-65.

ingly important place in the canonical collections which were to appear from this time on until the publication of the *Decretum Gratiani.* Nevertheless, though the authority of the Fathers was very great and their texts were used extensively in the canonical collections, the patristic writings were never given the force of law in the western Church.[13] For it is only in the *Decree of Gratian* that Canon Law appears for the first time as a law claiming universal validity.

[13] Van Hove, *Prolegomena,* p. 63.

CHAPTER III

DOCTRINAL INTERPRETATION IN THE PRE-CODE CANON LAW

ARTICLE I. NOTION OF DOCTRINAL INTERPRETATION

In the foregoing chapters consideration was given to the concept of interpretation in Roman Law, and in a much broader sense also to the effect which the Fathers of the Church exercised on the interpretation of ecclesiastical law. At this particular point a more precise consideration may be accorded to the history of doctrinal interpretation.

Accursius (1185-1260) in a gloss on the Digest Law, *"Si de interpretatione,"* indicated a fourfold division of interpretation: legislative, judicial, customary, and doctrinal.[1] This division was repeated in the Glossa to the decretal law *"Ad haec."*[2] The Glossators did not use these words specifically, but the ideas were the same. Thus interpretation of the law could be: 1) general and necessary and to be written down—as the interpretation of a ruler or a legislator; 2) general and necessary but not to be written—as the interpretation made by custom; 3) not general, but necessary and to be written down—as the interpretation made by a judge; 4) not general, nor necessary, nor to be written down, except for memory—as the interpretation made by teachers and doctors of the law. Suarez (1548-1617) reduced these to three, combining the first and third to denote authentic interpretation, with the second denoting the usual, and the fourth the doctrinal interpretation.[3] Doctrinal interpretation was the least important on the legislative scale. Nevertheless the interpretation of the legal expert was of great importance, and

[1] *Glossa* s. v. *Si de interpretatione,* D. (1. 3) 37.

[2] *Glossa* s. v. *Interpretatus,* c. 1. X, *de postulatione praelatorum,* 1. 5.

[3] Suarez, *Opera Omnia,* 28 vols., Vols. V-VI, *Tractatus de Legibus et Legislatore Deo* (ed. L. Vives, Parisiis, 1856-1861), *De Legibus,* Lib. VI, cap. I, n. 1.

was highly influential in the formation and development of law. It is with doctrinal interpretation that the discussion here is primarily concerned.

Doctrinal interpretation is almost universally admitted in all human laws whether civil or ecclesiastical. For it is almost impossible for a man to so express his meaning in all cases in terms so clear and concise that no ambiguities or doubts arise, especially since laws are usually brief in form and expressed in general words. To meet this necessity there developed the profession of lawyers and legal experts, whose chief function it was to discover the true meaning and the true interpretation of human laws.[4] Schmalzgrueber (1663-1735) noted that, since the legislator himself could not readily solve all these doubts, it was necessary that the function be given to the doctors of the law.[5] At times, doctrinal interpretation was for various reasons forbidden, as has been noted previously in the case of Justinian,[6] and in similar instances that will be noted later on in this study.

It seems indicated to furnish here a precise definition of law and an explanation regarding doctrinal interpretation along with the authority attaching thereto.

Law is defined by St. Thomas (1225-1274) as an ordinance in accordance with reason promulgated by the head of the community for the sake of the common welfare.[7] It is an ordinance: not a mere exhortation, but a real command which a subject is morally bound to obey. It must be in accordance with right reason, for if a law is not "reasonable, moral and just," it will have no binding force. It must be for the common good, since the power of making law is given to the superior not for his own good nor for the good of private individuals, but rather for that of the community. It must be made by the head of the community, that is, he must be the rightful superior, possessing such public authority as corresponds to the juridically perfect society

[4] Suarez, *ibid.*, n. 5.

[5] Schmalzgrueber, *Ius Ecclesiasticum Universum* (5 vols. in 12), Romae, 1843-1845), Lib. I, tit. II, n. 46.

[6] See page 9.

[7] *Summa Theologica,* Ia IIae, q. 90, art. 4, *in corpore.*

for which the law is enacted. Finally, it must be promulgated or made known to the subject before it can actually bind him.[8]

The lawmaker conceives an ordinance, decides to make that ordinance binding on his subjects, frames the idea in human language in order to transfer it to the minds of his subjects, promulgates the ordinance, and the result is law.

Doctrinal interpretation may be defined as a clearer determination of the mind or words of the legislator, which is not authoritative and therefore of itself not binding, but directive and based upon science, made according to a certain set of critical rules by those who are skilled in the art of jurisprudence.[9] It was the task of doctrinal interpretation to arrive at the true meaning of the law as intended by the legislator. The legal doctors had no authority to induce the obligation of law by their interpretation. This was the function of authentic interpretation. However, their interpretation furnished probability concerning the correct meaning of laws, as Accursius pointed out in his *Glossa* to the Digest Law, *"Si de interpretatione,"* cited above. Nevertheless, if all the doctors concurred in the interpretation of a law they produced moral certainty that this was the correct interpretation, not because they had any power over the law, but because their general agreement indicated a common acceptance of the law in that sense. Therefore Benedict XIV (1740-1758) remarked that whoever had followed his own opinion in ecclesiastical trials instead of the common teaching of the jurists would undoubtedly be compelled by the Church to conform to this common opinion.[10] Suarez and Schmalzgrueber stated that one could hardly have a safe conscience in following a contrary opinion.[11] Reiffenstuel (1642-1703) taught that the

[8] Cicognani, *Canon Law* (2. ed. Reprint, Westminster, Maryland: The Newman Press, 1949), pp. 522-524.

[9] Merkelbach, *Summa Theologiae Moralis* (2. ed., 3 vols., Parisiis: Typis Desclée, De Brouwer et Soc., 1935-1936), I, 263.

[10] *Ep. Redditae Nobis,* 5 dec., 1744, § 8—*Codicis Iuris Canonici Fontes* (cura Emi Petri Card. Gasparri editi, 9 vols., Romae [later Civitate Vaticana], Typis Polyglottis Vaticanis, 1923-1939; Vols. VII, VIII, IX, ed. cura et studio Emi Iustinani Card. Serédi), n. 350 (hereafter cited *Fontes*).

[11] Suarez, *De Legibus,* Lib. VI, cap. I, n. 6; Schmalzgrueber, *op. cit.,* Lib. I, tit. II, n. 44.

doctrinal interpretation needed to be followed if no better foundation of law was at hand.[12] If however these experts disagreed among themselves, then the intrinsic worth of the reasons given and the greater or lesser authority enjoyed by this or that particular doctor were the elements which would decide what interpretation was the more probably true one. Their reason therefore had to be based on the accepted rules of jurisprudence developed by the jurists through the centuries, because, as Reiffenstuel insisted, rules were formed for the reason namely that the doctors might be aided in their task of finding the intention or the mind of the legislator through the words expressed in his laws.[13]

The Glossators, in view of their deep knowledge of Roman Law and their classic interpretation of it, gained special authority as doctrinal interpreters. Accursius, the most famous glossator on the *Corpus Iuris Civilis,* has been said to have possessed greater authority than the text itself. This however is highly disputed.[14] The *Glossa Ordinaria* to the Decretals retained greater authority than any other, and no departure was admitted except for very good reasons.[15] At length in Italy and Germany the dictum was: "What the gloss does not permit the curia refuses." [16]

Article II. Primary Rules to Be Followed in Doctrinal Interpretation

In order that the law might be more safely interpreted, numerous rules based upon both Roman and Canon Law were proposed by the doctors in aid of those upon whom the task of interpretation fell.[17] There were two fundamental rules, one based on the words of the law, and the other based on the mind

[12] *Ius Canonicum Universum* (ed. novissima, 5 vols., Romae, 1831-1834), Lib. I, tit. II, n. 364.

[13] Reiffenstuel, *op. cit.,* Lib. I, tit. II, nn. 382-383.

[14] Sherman, *Roman Law in the Modern World* (2. ed., 3 vols., New York: Baker, Voorhis, & Co., 1924), sect. 213.

[15] Reiffenstuel, *op. cit. Prooemium,* nn. 147-149.

[16] Cicognani, *op. cit.,* p. 327.

[17] Schmalzgrueber, *op. cit.,* Lib. I, tit. II, nn. 46-47.

of the legislator. Just which of these was primary is not easy to decide, since emphasis seemed to be placed first on the one and then on the other, as will be noted subsequently. It is true that the law had to be interpreted according to the mind of the legislator, but the mind of the legislator was ordinarily discovered from the wording of the law. Accordingly it appears that the first fundamental rule of interpretation was to be based upon the meaning of the words.

Section 1. First General Rule

Words were to be understood according to their proper signification unless another meaning was indicated by the subject matter or the nature of the act or contract.[18] Suarez remarked that it was through the words of the law that one arrived at a knowledge of the mind of the legislator, and that, if other means such as mere conjecture were used, men would often fall into error.[19] The word "proper" was used to indicate the customary signification of the term, namely that meaning which customary use had attached to the word, and not the meaning that was based on the opinions of individuals.[20]

Bartolus A. Saxoferrato (1314-1359) very insistently warned that in the interpretation of words the proper signification was to be followed.[21] If a word had a number of proper significations, then, according to the Digest law, *"Quotiens,"* there was to be preferred the meaning which more suitably fitted the subject matter.[22] If a word had a proper and an improper meaning, the proper meaning was to be taken.[23] Sometimes it happened that the common usage had changed the original meaning of a word

[18] Reiffenstuel, *op. cit.,* Lib. I, tit. II, n. 390.

[19] *De Legibus,* Lib. VI, cap. I, n. 15.

[20] "... non enim ex opinionibus singulorum, sed ex communi usu nomina exaudiri debere." D. (33. 10) (7. 2).

[21] *Omnia Quae Extant Opera* (10 vols., sexta editio, Venetiis, 1590-1615), I, *Commentaria* in ff. *De Iustitia et Iure,* 1. *Omnes populi* (D. [1, 1] 9), nn. 53-58.

[22] "Quotiens idem sermo duas sententias exprimit, ea potissimum excipiatur quae rei gerendae aptior est."—D. (50, 17) 67.

[23] Bartolus, *loc. cit.*

and substituted a figurative one. In this case the figurative meaning really obtained as the common meaning, and that was then to be taken.[24]

Again, a word could have a natural signification based upon common usage, and a civil or legal signification which arose through a fiction of law. For example, death according to the common acceptance of the word meant physical death, whereas by a fiction of law it could mean religious profession or exile. Here too the natural signification had to be taken unless there was no doubt that the civil signification was intended. An example of this is had in the glossa to the decretal law *"Ad audientiam."* The Glossator, in commenting on the word *"labores"* stated that without certain knowledge one was not to recede from the form of the words.[25]

Joannes Andreae (1272-1348) in his comment on the Decretal *Susceptum* of Boniface VIII noted that the words *"per resignationem"* and *"per mortem"* were to be taken in their natural meaning.[26] However there were cases in which the law itself had invented certain words for a proper use. An example of these were such terms as *"excommunicatio," "censura."* These had to be understood according to their legal meaning, for that was their natural meaning as created by law.[27]

It is to be noted that the second part of this fundamental rule of interpretation allowed for some exceptions. When the intention of the author was clearly indicated by the subject matter or the nature of the act or contract, and this demanded a signification of the word other than the proper one, a departure from the proper signification became necessary. This happened

[24] *Glossa* s. v. *Ex communi usu:* "Scilicet, proprio aut figurato, nam et figurativa significatio communis est et sic usitata potest appellari." D. (33, 10) (7. 2).

[25] *Glossa* s. v. *Intellegeremus,* ad c. 12, X, *de decimis primitiis, et oblationibus,* III, 30—"argumentum quod a forma verborum sine certa scientia non est recedendum."

[26] *Glossa* s. v. *Humanis,* ad c. *de rescriptis,* I, 3, in VI°.—"Solvitur de propria significatione vocabuli . . . non sic in propria significatione dicitur 'renuntiasse' qui mortuus est, cum resignatio sit voluntaria, illa coacta."

[27] Suarez, *De Legibus,* Lib. VI, cap. I, n. 10.

more often in respect of particular laws and contracts. Sometimes the custom or the usage in one region had perhaps changed the ordinary signification of a word and attached to it another meaning. Then, as Bartolus noted, the custom of that region was to be followed in the interpretation of its particular laws.[28] There are numerous examples in the Digest law which show how custom, circumstances, and subject matter demanded another signification.[29]

Again, words had to be interpreted in such a way that the matter at hand prevailed rather than perished.[30] This rule was repeated by the Glossator in his comment on the decretal law *"Cum super."*[31] Finally, words were not to be interpreted in the proper sense if such an interpretation led to an absurdity. The decretal law *"Solitae"* furnished a rather lengthy example of this.[32]

It is evident that words were to be interpreted in their context. It is only by examining words in their context that one could apply the above mentioned rules. From the context it was seen whether the word was to be taken in its natural or legal sense, whether it should be interpreted properly or improperly, or perhaps figuratively according to the demands of custom, circumstances and the subject matter. The Digest law warned against interpreting words out of their context,[33] and the

[28] Bartolus, *ibid.*, n. 58: "Vel si communis usus loquendi aliter se haberet."

[29] "Optimum ergo esse Pedius ait non propriam verborum significationem scrutari, sed in primis quid testator demonstrare voluerit, deinde in qua praesumptione sunt qui in quaque regione commorantur." D. (33, 7) (18, 3); "Si numerus nummorum legatus sit, neque apparet, quales sunt legati, ante omnia ipsius patrisfamilias consuetudo, deinde regionis, in qua versatus est, expuirenda est; sed et mens patrisfamilias et legatarii dignitas vel caritas et necessitudo, item earum quae praecedunt vel quae sequuntur summarum scripta sunt spectanda." D. (33, 7) 18, 3. Other examples are found in D. (19, 2) (15, 4); D. (35, 1) 9.

[30] C. (5. 13) (1. 1).

[31] *Glossa* s. v. *Mutuo advers.*, c. 23, X, *de officio et potestate iudicis delegati,* I, 29: " . . . res de qua agitur potius valeat quam pereat."

[32] C. 6, X, *de maioritate et obedientia,* I, 33.

[33] "Incivile est nisi tota lege perspecta una aliqua particula eius proposita iudicare vel respondere."—D. (1. 3) 24.

Glossator explained that the earlier part could be corrected by a following part.[34] Words could have a variety of meanings in different contexts, and the important thing was to determine the exact meaning intended by the author in each particular instance.

This general principle was reflected as the common teaching of the doctors of law.[35] The reason for it is evident. If a lawmaker wished his laws to be effective, he had to use clear words, words in their proper signification. Otherwise laws would become the occasion for many disputes and much quarreling.[36]

Section 2. Second General Rule

Interpretation was to conform rather to the intent than to the words of the law.[37]

As noted in the preceding section, ordinarily the words in their proper signification served to reveal the intention of the legislator. Sometimes, however, circumstances indicated that the signification of the words was to be changed for a proper conformity to the intention of the legislator. The question whether greater emphasis was to be attached to the words or to the intent had long been a matter of dispute. This had obtained even in early Roman Law.[38] All agreed that it was the very purpose of interpretation to arrive at the mind and the will of the legislator, but they differed on the specific means that was to receive primary attention. Even the laws themselves as well as the commentators seemed at times to stress one element, and at other times another.

[34] *Glossa* s. v. *Incivile* D. (1. 3) 24: " . . . nam plerumque principium per finem corrigitur."

[35] Barbosa, *Tractatus Varii* (Lugduni, 1660), *Axiomata,* Axioma 222, n. 4; Tuschus, *Practicae Conclusiones Iuris in Omni Fori Frequentiores* (8 vols., Lugduni, 1634; Add. Vol. IX, Lugduni, 1670), VIII, Litt. V, conc. 91 (hereafter cited *Practicae Conclusiones*); Suarez, *loc. cit.;* Reiffenstuel, Lib. I, tit. II, n. 390; Schmalzgrueber, Lib. I, tit. II, n. 47.

[36] Reiffenstuel, *loc. cit.*

[37] "Interpretatio potius menti quam verbis convenire debet."—Reiffenstuel, Lib. I, tit. II, n. 386.

[38] See pages 7-8.

The Digest law *"Scire leges"* warned that a true understanding of the law consisted rather in the knowledge of the sense of the law than in just a mere adherence to the words.[39] The Code of Justinian stated that if one interpreted the words of the law against its purpose one is guilty of a violation of the law.[40] This same principle was repeated in the Rules of Law of Boniface VIII.[41] It was understood however that the intention of the legislator was sufficiently known to indicate the sense in which the words were to be understood. This is seen in the Glossa to the law *"Humanae aures."* Though the canon itself stated that the words must be subservient to the intention, and not the intention to the words,[42] yet the Glossator noted that this was true only when clear knowledge of the intention was had. Otherwise, when some doubt obtained, one was not to depart from the words.[43]

The decretal law *"In his"* furnished an authentic interpretation based on this same principle.[44] The following law under the same title gave further instruction on how to discover the intention of the lawgiver, namely from the reasons for his statement, which could help to clarify the meaning of ambiguous words.[45] The Glossa to the word *"Intelligentia"* repeated that

[39] "Scire leges non hoc est verba earum tenere, sed vim ac potestatem."—D. (1, 3) 17. The *Glossa* s. v. *Scire leges,* ". . . Tria attendes verba et vim, id est proprium sensum et potestatem."

[40] "Non dubium est in legem committere eum, qui verba legis amplexus contra legis nititur voluntatem."—C. (1, 14) 5.

[41] Reg. 88, R. J., in VI°: "Certum est, quod is committit in legem, qui legis verba complectens, contra legis nititur voluntatem."

[42] "Humanae aures verba nostra talia iudicant, qualia foris sonant . . . quia non debet aliquis verba considerare, sed voluntatem et intentionem, quia non debet intentio verbis deservire, sed verba intentioni."—C. 11, C. XXII, q. 5.

[43] *Glossa* s. v. *Verba,* ad. C. 11, C. XXII, q. 5: ". . . potius consideranda est mens alicuius quam verba. . . . Sed hoc verum est cum constat de intellectu. Alias in dubiis a verbis non est recedendum."

[44] ". . . non debet aliquis considerare verba, sed voluntatem, cum non intentio verbis, sed verba intentioni debent deservire."—C. 15, X, *de verborum significatione,* V, 40.

[45] "Intelligentia dictorum ex causis est assumenda dicendi, quia non sermoni res, sed rei est sermoni subiectus."—C. 6, *ibid.*

the words are subservient to the intention, and not the intention to the words.[46] Again, the Glossa to the words *"Ex causis"* of the same law stated that words were not immediately at their face value to be understood as they sounded, especially when they were ambiguous, but rather the intent was to be considered.[47]

A few remarks on the relationship between words and intention seem appropriate at this point. It seems that in the interpretation of law the words should be considered first, because, as Suarez maintained, in the promulgation of law the mind and the intention of the legislator is first made known to the subject through the words of the law.[48] Tuschus (1534-1620) taught the same thing in some of his conclusions, namely that the intention was to be gathered from the words, and therefore the words introduced to us the mind of the legislator, since the mind was presumed to be what the words demonstrated.[49] On the other hand, if the law remained doubtful, then the first step in interpretation was recourse to the mind of the legislator, as was pointed out in the Glossa to the decretal law *"Intelligentia."* Tuschus also in one of his conclusions held this principle.[50] How then was the mind of the legislator to be discovered? According to Reiffenstuel the mind was to be discovered from the subject matter of the law, from the circumstances, and especially from the reason of the law, if it was contained in the law. However, he again called attention to the fact that the words necessarily occupied the first place.[51] Suarez was of the same opinion.[52]

[46] ". . . non tantum ipsa significatio verborum, sed etiam causae dicendi debent considerari, quia verba deserviunt intentioni, et non intentio verbis." —*Loc. cit.*

[47] *Glossa* s. v. *Ex causis* ". . . non statim debemus intelligere ut verba prima facie sonare videntur, maxime ubi ambigua sunt, sed debemus recurrere ad intentionem loquentis."—*Loc. cit.*

[48] Suarez, *De Legibus,* Lib. VI, cap. I, n. 15.

[49] Tuschus, *Praticae Conclusiones,* V, Litt. M, conc. 198, n. 1, n. 90, and nn. 91-95.

[50] *Ibid.,* concl. 199: "Mens et ratio, attenda, plus quam verba."

[51] *Ius Canonicum Universum,* Lib. I, tit. II, nn. 387-389.

[52] *De Legibus,* Lib. VI, cap. II, n. 20: "Ratio motiva legis, quae si in ipsa lege contineatur, magnum habet indicium legislatoris."

Accordingly the "reason of the law" will be considered in the next section as the third general principle of doctrinal interpretation.

Section 3. Third General Rule

When the reason of law is the same, the disposition of the law is the same.[53]

The third rule of interpretation, after a contemplation of the words and the intention, looked to the purpose of or the reason for the law. It was an axiom among doctrinal interpreters that the reason for a law was the soul of the law. It should be called to attention here that the words, the mind of the legislator, the intention of the legislator, and the reason for the law, inasmuch as they were so closely interrelated, were often used indiscriminately by the Glossators and the authors. This is easily understood. The reason of the law was included in the mind of the legislator, which in turn was included in his intention. Suarez explained this by saying that there are two distinct elements in the mind of the legislator, namely, his will or intention by which he wishes to command, and the reason by which he is moved, and in these two things consists the soul of the law.[54]

It was also necessary to distinguish a twofold reason for a law. One could be called the motivating cause, and this was extrinsic to the law; the other could be called the final cause, which was intrinsic to the law. Accordingly two different legislators could have different motivating causes for passing the same law, though its final cause was the same. Thus one legislator could impose the law of fasting as a means of satisfaction for sin, and another, the same law as a means of fostering mortification, whereas the final cause or the juridic reason for the fasting inhered in the desired acquisition of the virtue of temperance.[55] In the doctrinal interpretation of law, "reason" was used in this latter sense, that is, as the final cause, or the intrinsic motive, or simply the reason for the law, since this reason was sometimes mentioned in the law itself or could be deduced at times from

[53] "Ubi eadem est ratio, eadem est iuris dispositio."—Reiffenstuel, Lib. I, tit. II, n. 410; Barbosa, *Tractatus Varii, Axiomata,* Axioma 197, n. 3.

[54] *De Legibus,* Lib. III, cap. 21, n. 1.

[55] Suarez, *loc. cit.*

the law, whereas at best a probable conjecture, if any, could be made as to the reason that actually motivated the legislator in making the laws. Therefore Baldus de Ubaldis (1327-1400) stated that knowledge of the final cause of the law could be used as a basis for the interpretation of law, but not knowledge of the impulsive cause.[56] In his explanation, Tuschus asserted that the purpose of the law and its final cause are one and the same, and that this is the soul of the law.[57] Reiffenstuel acknowledged this assertion as an accepted maxim among the doctors.[58] The purpose of the law therefore indicated the mind of the legislator, and helped the interpreter to understand what the words of the law meant. Thus it is seen that the reason for the law was closely related to the second general rule, which concerned the mind of the legislator.

A complete exposition of this general rule would prove overlengthy for this brief historical study. While most of the authors agreed on the general principle, the variety of explanations and applications of it was very great. Therefore it will be sufficient here to consider briefly the sources of this principle, and to note some of the main points of the controversy.

The Digest law "*Illud*" directed that the same application of the law be used in the "*actio damni*" as in the "*actio furti,*" since the same reason of law was found in both.[59] Accordingly the Glossator concluded that, when the reason of law was the same, the law itself was the same.[60] It must be observed here that a real identity of reason existed in this case, and not just a similarity; and, secondly, this identity of reason was given in the case as a guide for the judge as to what law should be used in this action. This will be explained later.

The Glossator of the Decretal Law "*Saepe contingit,*" in a case

[56] *In Decretalium Volumen Commentaria* (Venetiis, 1580), Lib. I, tit. II, cap. 1, n. 53.

[57] "Ratio legis et causa finalis sunt unum et idem, prout mens et ratio sunt unum et idem."—*Op. cit.,* VI, Litt. R. concl. 30, n. 4; ". . . est enim ratio anima legis et statuti."—*Loc. cit.*

[58] *Op. cit.,* Lib. I, tit. II, n. 388.

[59] D. (9, 2) 32.

[60] *Ibid., Glossa* s. v. *Existimari:* "Notandum quod ubi est eadem ratio est idem ius."

wherein the same law was applied in a similar case, pointed out that the same reason and a genuine similarity existed.[61] Another Decretal law, *"Inter corporalia,"* solved a case and gave as its principle that the same judgment must be applied in similar cases.[62] The Glossa to this law cited a canon from the *Decretum* as an objection to this principle, inasmuch as in that canon a similar application of law was not allowed in similar cases.[63] However the objection was not a valid one, since in the canon the similarity of reason was only apparent. Nevertheless there was still the problem whether an identity of reason had to be present for the application of the same law in like cases.

This difficulty was solved by Suarez when he pointed out that a similarity of reason was enough for a judge in applying the law to a case not covered by the law, but that it was not sufficient for inducing a moral obligation for a person or a group of persons if it implied nothing more than the existence of a similar person or group of persons with the same kind of obligation.[64] The first part of this opinion stood confirmed by the Digest law *"Nam ut ait,"* which recommended an extension of the law, by one who at least had jurisdiction, to cases which reflected the same utility. The procedure lay from one similar case to another, as the Glossa noted.[65]

The second part of Suarez's opinion, namely, that a mere similarity of reason did not necessarily signify an intention on the part of the legislator to induce an obligation in similar cases, was insinuated in two decretal laws with their glosses. The

[61] *Glossa* s. v. *Italia,* ad c. 1. *de temporibus ordinationum et qualitate ordinandorum,* I, 9, in VI°: "Cum post omnia sit eadem ratio utrobique; ergo idem ius, nec videtur ista applicatio vel extensio . . . ubi enim est eadem ratio et omnimoda similitudo, non proprie dicimus extendere."

[62] ". . . cum de similibus idem iudicium sit habendum."—C. 2, X, *de translatione episcopi,* I, 7.

[63] *Glossa* s. v. *Similitudinem,* ad c. 41, C. XXVII, q. 1.

[64] *De Legibus,* Lib. VI, cap. III, nn. 9-11.

[65] "Nam, ut aut Pedius, quotiens lege aliquid unum vel alterum introductum est, bona occasio est cetera, quae tendunt ad eandem utilitatem, vel interpretatione vel certe iurisdictione suppleri."—D. (1, 3) 13; *Glossa* s. v. *Suppleri:* "procedendo de similibus ad similia."

decretal law "*Non solum*" prohibited the Order of Preachers and the Friars Minor from admitting anyone to profession until after a year's probation.[66] Later Boniface VIII, by the law "*Constitutionem,*" extended the law to the other Mendicant Orders. The Glossa added that, if the pope had not passed this law, it would not have existed for them, even though the reason for it was similar.[67]

It seems safe to state it as the common opinion of the doctors that generally, when an identity of reason existed, the law was to be extended to the persons and cases covered by that reason. But they differed as to the conditions required for the extension, and also as to whether the reason had to be expressed in the law or not.

Tuschus held that when the reason for the law was expressed in the law, the law applied to all cases in which that reason existed, and also when only one reason could be assigned for the law, even though this was not expressed, the law operated as if it had been expressed.[68]

Panormitanus (1386-1453) maintained that, if the reason of the law was in evidence, then, whenever there was an identity of reason, the law was to be extended even in penalties. For the words of the law were restricted and extended to the limits of the reason of the law. If the reason was not expressed but self-evident, then the law extended as far as the reason extended.[69]

[66] C. 2, *de regularibus et transeuntibus ad religionem,* III, 14, in VI°.

[67] ". . . Unde nos pari similititudine rationis inducti, declarationem eandem ad aliorum Mendicantium ordines prorogamus."—C. 3, *de regularibus et transeuntibus ad religionem,* III, 14, in VI°. The *Glossa* s. v. *Prorogamus:* ". . . Dico quod hic Bonifatius non dixit declaramus, sed prorogamus: unde licet eadem ratio esset in aliis Mendicantibus, quae in Praedicatoribus atque Minoribus: tamen constitutio illa (*Non solum*) *non* extenderetur ad illos, nisi hic per Bonifatium prorogata fuisset."

[68] "Nisi ratio sit expressa, quia tunc bene fit extensio, ubi ratio expressa militat, quia lex dicitur etiam in eo sensu loqui."—*Practicae Conclusiones,* concl. 31, n. 44. "Ratio unica legis quando potest assignari, licet non sit expressa, tamen idem operatur, ac si esset expressa."—*Ibid.,* concl. 30, n. 5, and concl. 31, n. 17.

[69] "Sed mihi placet, quod ubi potest apparere de ratione legis, quod tunc ex identitate rationis debet extendi, etiam quoad poenam. . . . Unde quemadmodum corpus regularitur ab anima, ita et ipsa lex regulariter a ratione

On the other hand, Suarez held that generally the reason of a law had to be written in the law before the law could be extended to other cases, especially in the case of an obligation imposed upon others. Nevertheless he noted that sometimes the reason, even though not expressed in the law, could be so evident or so commonly acknowledged that it proved sufficient for inducing the obligation of the law.[70] However, Suarez maintained that the law could not be extended to any case just on account of the identity of reason. He further insisted that the reason for the law had to be adequate to the law, namely that the reason was the only one intended by the law, that it alone sufficiently and efficaciously moved the legislator to enact the law, and that the words of the law at least in a wide and improper sense had to allow for the extension, or that some other necessity such as an injustice or absurdity in the law demanded it.[71] He proved his position by stating that the intention of the legislator had no legal force unless it was in some way expressed in the words of the law, and at the same time the reason of the law had to be adequate to the law, otherwise one could not be certain that the legislator wanted to include all for whom the same reason of the law existed.[72]

Reiffenstuel stated the principle of the third general rule of

---

legis et non a verbis. Nam verba legis restringuntur et ampliantur ad limites rationis ipsius legis."—Lib. I, tit. III (*de rescriptis*), cap. *Quia nonnulli,* n. 10, in *Omnia Quae Extant Commentaria in Decretales* (6 vols., Venetiis, 1588). (Hereafter cited *Commentaria.*)

[70] *De Legibus,* Lib. VI, cap. IV, n. 6.

[71] *Ibid.,* cap. III, nn. 16-22.

[72] *Ibid.,* cap. I, n. 13; cap. III, n. 19: ". . . licet in aliis casibus inveniatur eadem ratio, non potest ex illa inferre fuisse comprehensos sub mente legislatoris, quia potuit non moveri ad illos, ex defectu aliarum rationum vel circumstantiarum." Also cap. III, n. 16: ". . . Hanc assertionem pono propter sententiam valde communem asserentem ex identitate rationis extendendam esse legem, quam in aliquo sensu veram esse negare non possimus. . . . Secundo, propter varia iura quae hoc indicant, quanquam (si attente expendantur) fere nunquam separet omnino rationem a verbis, quia non colligent ex identitate rationis mentem legislatoris fuisse comprehendere aliquam casum non satis expressum in verbis, nisi vel extendendo verba in aliqua significatione saltem lata, vel impropria, vel quia alia necessitas cogit, ut quod alias lex esset iniusta, vel absurda."

law, and explained that the reason had to be the adequate final cause without any apparent disparity.[73]

Schmalzgrueber felt that on intrinsic grounds a law could not be extended, in consideration simply of a similarity or identity of reason, to a case which was not comprehended in the words of the law. But he stated that the extension could be permitted if such an extension was presumed to be according to the mind of the legislator, for example, in correlative cases, or when an injustice or absurdity would otherwise result from the law. He also allowed a judge in reaching a verdict to proceed according to similarities.[74]

The disagreement among the authors consisted in this: some allowed an extension of the law in the face simply of an identity of reason, whereas others demanded more. Most of the doctors who under either form held this principle taught that there was question properly not of an extension of the law but of a comprehension. Thus Barbosa (1589-1649) declared that the existence of the same reason implied the existence of the same law, not extensively but comprehensively.[75] In order to understand this it is necessary to observe that many authors distinguished two kinds of extension: extension properly so called, or "*mere extensiva*," and improperly so called, or "*comprehensiva*." The first was an extension of the law not only beyond the words of the law but even beyond the mind of the legislator, though not contrary to his mind. The second was an extension of the law beyond the words but not beyond the mind of the legislator.[76]

The common opinion is found expressed in Reiffenstuel. A purely extensive doctrinal interpretation transcended the scope and the reach of the law, and therefore the legislator needed first to accept it and promulgate it before it became law, whereas a comprehensive interpretation pointed to an extension that with probability reflected the actual law. He called the comprehen-

[73] Lib. I, tit. II, n. 410.

[74] Lib. I, tit. II, n. 48.

[75] *Tractatus Varii, Axiomata,* Axioma 197, n. 7: "Ubi est eadem ratio, dicatur adesse eadem lex, non extensive, sed comprehensive."

[76] Reiffenstuel, Lib. I, tit. II, nn. 371-376; Suarez, *De Legibus,* Lib. VI, cap. III, n. 9.

sive extension a declaration of the law rather than an extension of it.[77] Suarez contended that, if the reason for the law was in itself expressed in the law, then this third general principle seemed right after the words of the law to occupy second place in the general rules of interpretation.[78]

[77] *Loc. cit.*

[78] "At vero quando ratio legis in ipsa lege continetur, magnum indicium esse potest mentis legislatoris, et post verba ipsa videtur secundum certitudinis locum obtinere."—*De Legibus,* Lib. VI, cap. I, n. 20. This is also noted by Tuschus, *op. cit.*, VI, Litt. R, concl. 32, n. 1, and by Reiffenstuel, *ibid.*, n. 376.

CHAPTER IV

SECONDARY RULES OF DOCTRINAL INTERPRETATION

Article I. General Rules

The three general rules enumerated in the preceding chapter formed the backbone of doctrinal interpretation, since they contained the three principal elements involved, namely, the words of the law, the mind of the legislator, and the purpose of the law. Besides these there obtained many secondary rules which, when used in conjunction with the principal rules, were often of considerable assistance in the doctrinal interpretation of law. A few of the more important ones will be delineated here.

Section 1. Burdens Are to Be Restricted and Favors Extended [1]

In favorable laws the words, if obscure, were to be interpreted in their broadest sense, not however in odious matters. It is readily seen, nevertheless, that this rule was to be taken in conjunction with the third rule of interpretation, the identity of the reason for the law, since the doctrinal interpreter could neither extend nor restrict the law, except in accordance with the mind of the legislator, that is, only a comprehensive extension or restriction was allowed.

The Digest law stated that in doubts the more favorable interpretation was to be preferred.[2] In the very same title this principle was again stated, this time in favor of liberty.[3] Another Digest law pointed out that in penal matters a benign rather than a harsh interpretation was to be applied.[4]

[1] "Odia restringi et favores convenit ampliari."—Reg. 15, R. J., in VI°.

[2] "Semper in dubiis benigniora praeferenda sunt."—D. (50, 17) 56.

[3] "Quotiens dubia interpretatio libertatis est, secundum libertatem respondendum erit."—D. (50, 17) 20.

[4] "Interpretatione legum poenae molliendae sunt potius quam asperandae." —D. (48, 19) 42.

This same principle was adopted in early Canon Law, and a very clear example is found in the decretal law *"Si sententia."* This law, in its reference to the penalty of interdict, stated that apart from an express statement to the contrary the word "clergy" did not include the "people," and, on the other hand, the word "people" did not include the "clergy," unless the interdict stated otherwise.[5] Reiffenstuel commented that in a favorable law the clergy would be included under the word "people." However, another decretal law at first glance seemed to contradict this one, stating that when a city was under interdict the suburbs also were included.[6] Yet there was no real contradiction, for in this case the circumstances were different, inasmuch as the law itself stated that, if the suburbs were not included, the interdict would be rendered useless and have no penal force.

How was this rule to be applied to a law which was partly favorable and partly odious? The Glossa to the law *"Venia"* in the Justinian Codex explained that in so far as it was odious it should be restricted, and in so far as it was favorable it should be extended.[7] Therefore Reiffenstuel taught that whenever the two cannot be separated in the law, the part which is favorable is to be broadly interpreted, and the odious part is strictly interpreted.[8] Benefices in the wide sense (not in the technical meaning of ecclesiastical benefices) were considered favors, and therefore were to be interpreted broadly. This is found in a Digest law referring to an imperial benefice.[9]

The same principle was accepted in Canon Law and is found

[5] C. 16, *de sententia excommunicationis, suspensionis et interdicti,* V, 11, in VI°: "Si sententia interdicti proferatur in clerum, non intelligitur, nisi aliud sit expressum in ea, interdictus populus; nec etiam e converso."

[6] C. 17, *de sententia excommunicationis, suspensionis et interdicti,* V. 11, in VI°.

[7] *Glossa* s. v. *Liberis,* C. (2, 2) 2: ". . . ex parte patroni est favor, et ideo prorogandus, ex parte liberti est odium, et ideo restringendum."

[8] Lib. I, tit. II, nn. 435-436.

[9] "Beneficium imperatoris, quod a divina scilicet eius indulgentia proficiscitur, quam plenissime interpretari debemus."—D. (1, 4) 3.

in the Decretal law *"Olim,"* but the Glossator added that it was not to be interpreted in such a way as to injure another.[10] Nevertheless Canon Law excepted one class of favors from a broad interpretation, namely, rescripts given for the obtaining of ecclesiastical benefices. These were looked upon as exceptions to the general rule, and were subject to a strict interpretation. The Decretal law *"Quamvis"* stated this exception and gave the reason—such rescripts could serve to foster untoward ambitions.[11]

Notwithstanding this general principle, sometimes an extension of the law seemed to be valid even in odious matters, namely when the identical reason as expressed in the law existed. It was a disputed question and formed part of the controversy concerning the extension of the law as based on the identity of reason for the law. As has been noted, Panormitanus seemed to hold that even in consideration simply of an identity of reason a law should be extended even in penal matters, for, as he said, the reason is the soul of the law and regulates the law.[12] Suarez also allowed for an extension in penal laws, but demanded more than an identity of reason, as has been seen previously.[13] Moreover, he also explained that a comprehensive extension could be twofold, one of necessity, the other of congruity. When it was a case of necessity, that is, when it was necessary to preserve the efficacy or justice of the law, then both penal as well as favorable laws were to be extended.[14] When it

[10] C. 16, X, *de verborum significatione,* V, 40, and the *Glossa* s. v. *Largissime.*

[11] "Quamvis plenissima sit alias in beneficiis interpretatio facienda: litterae tamen super obtinendis beneficiis debent, cum sint ambitiosae, restringi."—C. 4, *de praebendis et dignitatibus,* III, 4, in VI°.

[12] See p. 27.

[13] See p. 28.

[14] "Praeterea debet intelligi quando talis comprehensio ex vi rationis necessaria est ut vere et integre impleatur ratio legis, vel ut sit justa et rationabilis, ut explicatum est, tunc enim est evidens necessitas, quia non minus efficax et justa ac rationabilis debet esse lex poenalis quam quaelibet alia."—*De Legibus,* Lib. VI, cap. IV, n. 2.

was a case of congruity, that is, when the prudence and justice of the law could be maintained without extension, then penal laws were not to be extended.[15] Tuschus also held that a penal law could not be extended in view simply of an identity of reason.[16]

Laws contrary to the common law were subject to strict interpretation and were not to be extended. Thus Pope Gregory the Great (590-604), in a letter to Felix, a bishop in Sicily, explained the privilege which he had granted to Bishop Augustine in England, allowing the neophytes to contract marriage with blood relatives of the fourth degree. But this privilege was no longer to be valid in subsequent generations, since it was contrary to the common law, and the reason for the privilege no longer existed—namely a concession to the weakness of the pagans converted to Christianity.[17] The decretal law *"Is qui"* stated this principle and applied it to a particular case concerning a dispensation submitted for a decision.[18] The reason for such a strict interpretation inhered in the fact that the dispensation was given contrary to the common law and therefore it was an odious matter. This principle was easily deduced from Rules 15, 28, and 78 of the Rules of Law of Boniface VIII.[19]

[15] "Dico ergo generales illas regulas de non ampliandis legibus poenalibus intelligi de interpretatione (ut ita dicam) voluntaria, id est, sine qua potest conservari prudens dispositio et justitia legis, quia infra hanc latitudinem benigne semper est interpretanda lex poenalis."—*Ibid.*, n. 3.

[16] *Practicae Conclusiones,* VI, Litt. R, concl. 31, n. 43.

[17] C. 20, C. XXXV, q. 3; Jaffé, *Regista Pontificum Romanorum ab condita ecclesia ad annum post Christum natum* MCXCVIII (2. ed., G. Wattenbach, F. Kaltenbrunner, P. Ewald, S. Loewenfeld, 2 vols., Lipsiae, 1885-1888), J. E., n. 1843, resp. 6.

[18] ". . . nequit praetextu dispensationis huiusmodi (quam exorbitantem a iure oportet veluti odiosam restringi), nisi unicum beneficium obtinere . . ."—C. 1, *de filiis presbyterorum ordinandis vel non,* I, 11, in VI°.

[19] They are respectively: "Odia restringi et favores convenit ampliari."—Reg. 15, R. J., in VI°; "Quae a iure communi exorbitant, nequaquam ad consequentiam sunt trahenda."—Reg. 28, R. J., in VI°; "In argumentum trahi nequeunt, quae propter necessitatem aliquando sunt concessa."—Reg. 78, R. J., in VI°.

Section 2. General Terms Are to Be Understood Generally [20]

When a law was general and contained no exceptions, it extended to all particular cases which fell under the scope of the law. The Glossator in commenting on the Digest law *"De Pretio"* [21] made this observation: where the law does not distinguish, neither ought we to distinguish. This maxim has long since been canonized by the doctors of the law. Nevertheless an exception to this rule occurred when the general law was qualified or limited by another. In that situation all the cases which were covered by the second law were removed from the extension of the first. This principle was nicely expressed in the 34th Rule of Law of Boniface VIII, *"Generi per speciem derogatur,"* [22] which has also become a famous maxim with doctrinal interpreters.

Section 3. An Indefinite Term Is Equivalent to a Universal Term [23]

This rule was very closely related to the preceding one, and was partly based on the same reason. When the author of the law could have made an exception but did not, and instead used general or indefinite terms, it was presumed that he included all persons or things which fell within that classification. A celebrated case is found in the Digest law *"Si servitus,"* where a doubt was solved regarding the universal term "light." The lawmaker observed that, since no limitation was placed on the word "light," the term included all lights, both present and future.[24] The same principle is found later on in the Digest in

[20] "Verba generalia generaliter sunt intelligenda."—Reiffenstuel, Lib. I, tit. II, n. 398.

[21] D. (6, 2) 8.

[22] Reg. 34, R. J., in VI°.

[23] "Indefinita locutio aequipollet universali."—Reiffenstuel, Lib. I, tit. II, n. 400.

[24] "Si servitus imposita fuerit 'lumina quae nunc sunt, ut ita sint,' de futuris luminibus nihil cavere videtur: quod si ita cautum 'ne luminibus officiatur,' ambigua est scriptura, utrum ne his luminibus officiatur quae nunc sunt, an etiam his quae postea quoque fuerint: humanius est verbo generali omne lumen significari, sive quod in praesenti sive quod post tempus conventionis contigerit."—D. (8, 2) 23.

the law *"Si pluribus,"* where it was explained that the universal term "heir" includes all heirs, since no distinction was made.[25]

The Glossators to the *Decretum Gratiani* were quick to adopt this principle of interpretation in the solving of cases contained in the canons on which they were commenting. An example is found in the canon *"Si Romanorum."* There *"tempora"* was interpreted to mean *"omnia tempora."*[26] Again in the decretal law *"Quia circa"* one finds an application of the same principle. The case in question was one wherein the terms relating to the granting of a benefice were called into doubt. Pope Innocent III (1198-1216) in his solution of the case stated that, since an exception could have been made and none was actually made, and since a broad interpretation should be allowed in the matter of benefices, and since one and the same concern should not be judged by different laws, it was to be concluded that the privilege included all tithes not only of the present but of the future as well.[27]

Reiffenstuel, in his commentary upon this rule, argued that an indefinite term was not really equivalent to a universal term, but became equivalent to a universal term from a benign interpretation of the mind of the legislator. This seemed evident in the example of the decretal law *"Quia circa"* just cited. Therefore he concluded that this rule was valid only when the same reason existed in all the cases included in the indefinite term.[28]

It is therefore to be noted that this rule could not be applied independently, but in conjunction with what was said before with reference to the three primary rules of interpretation. The Roman law *"Si servitus,"* quoted above, certainly considered

[25] D. (31) 44.

[26] C. 1, Dist. XIX, and the *Glossa* s. v. *Diversis:* ". . . notandum quod verbum indefinite prolatum generaliter est intelligendum."

[27] ". . . Quum nihil exceperit et poterit excepisse, ac in beneficiis plenissima sit interpretatio adhibenda, nec debeat una eademque substantia diverso iure censeri, intellexisse videtur non solum de decimis possessionum illius temporis, sed futuri."—C. 22, X, *de privilegiis et excessibus privilegiatorum,* V. 33, and the *Glossa* s. v. *Indefinite:* ". . . argumentum quod indefinite aequipollet universali."

[28] Reiffenstuel, Lib. I, tit. II, nn. 400-402.

other factors. The rule therefore did not hold unless the same reason and condition were found in the different cases. There were many examples of this contingency in Roman law. In the matter of legacies the indefinite word "wool" was taken to mean "crude wool" and not dyed wool.[29] In another matter relative to legacies the indefinite word "marble" was taken to mean only "crude marble" and not any finished product made of marble, since it was evident from the context of the will that a separate provision had been made for the finished products.[30]

Section 4. Effect of New Laws on Previous Laws

A short statement seems in place here regarding the relationship between prior general laws and the new general laws. If the new law explicitly, or even implicitly but clearly, abrogated the old law, there was no difficulty, for then the new law had to be observed. This obtained when the new law expressly mentioned the old law and declared that it was abrogated, or when the new law was entirely contrary to the old law. In cases of doubt, the principle that had been followed from time immemorial was that the old law was presumed to remain unchanged. This was also based on the principle that a change in the law was regarded an odious matter, and therefore the presumption stood in favor of the continuance of the old law.[31]

ARTICLE II. SPECIFIC RULES

The basic rules of interpretation as delineated previously governed all laws whether they were universal or general, particular or special. However, there were also some specific rules which had to be applied in the interpretation of dispensations, privileges and rescripts. Most of these rules were simply logical applications of the preceding general rules.

Section 1. Dispensations

The general rule on the interpretation of dispensations was that a dispensation implied an exemption from the law and

[29] D. (32) 70.

[30] D. (32) 100.

[31] Reiffenstuel, Lib. I, tit. II, nn. 419-420.

therefore was deemed an odious matter. Accordingly a granted dispensation was subject to a strict interpretation. For whatever was contrary to the common law was subject to a strict interpretation, as was noted previously. The decretal law *"Is qui"* explicitly applied this principle to dispensations from the common law.[32] However, governing the interpretation of dispensations there were two other principles which must not be overlooked. First, a dispensation from the principal thing was considered as extending to all accessory matters which were necessarily connected with or followed from the principal thing. The Glossator to the decretal law *"Si quis in clero"* affirmed this principle. The law mentioned the penalty incurred by clerics through their absence from or non residence at a church. The Glossator asked the question: does one, if by dispensation he has several churches or prebends and therefore must necessarily be absent from some of them incur this penalty? The response was in the negative, inasmuch as such a cleric was also dispensed from the law of residence at those other churches.[33]

Secondly, the delegated power of dispensing was to be interpreted widely, if the exercise of this power was not prejudicial to anyone but the delegator himself, since then it stood as a favorable matter. An example of this principle is seen in the decretal law *"Mandato,"* where the delegated power of dispensing monks guilty of simony was extended to include abbots guilty of the same crime, though no mention was made of this authority in the delegated power.[34] For this reason, canonists considered such grants of dispensatory power as exceptions to

[32] C. 1, *de filiis presbyterorum ordinandis vel non,* I, II, in VI°. See p. 34.

[33] C. 29, C. VII, q. 1, and the *Glossa* s. v. *Solemnibus.*

[34] C. 46, X, *de simonia et ne aliquid pro spiritulibus exigatur vel promittatur,* V. 3: ". . . dicimus mandatum Apostolicum etiam ad abbates extendi." Fagnanus, *Commentaria Super Quinque Libros Decretalium* (5 vols., Romae, 1661), Lib. V, tit. 3, dicto cap *Mandato,* n. 33: ". . . etsi dispensatio ipsa tamquam vulnerans ius commune sit odiosa et stricte accipienda . . . tamen dispensandi potestas, quae nulli est praeiudicialis, nisi ipsi concedenti, est favorabilis et late interpretanda, ut efficaciter probat haec Decretalis inducendo eam."

the general rule, since they proceeded from the liberality of the legislator.[35]

Section 2. Rescripts and Privileges

In general, the rules of interpretation just reviewed also governed the interpretation of rescripts and privileges. Summarily, in all rescripts and privileges the interpretation had to be made according to the proper signification of the words, if they were clear.[36] In a case of doubt, rescripts of justice had to be strictly interpreted according to the common law, since they sought and called for the observance of the common law. The decretal law *"Causam,"* in treating of a rescript of justice, commanded a strict adherence to the words of the rescript.[37] The Glossator in his *Casus* to this law noted that in the interpreting of the rescript one was not to depart from the common law, unless it was evident that the pope so wished.[38] Schmalzgrueber repeated this same principle.[39]

Beneficial grants which did not injure another's rights or another law were deemed to be of a favorable character, and therefore were to be widely interpreted.[40]

Rescripts for obtaining ecclesiastical benefices were to be strictly interpreted, since they could serve to foster untoward ambitions.[41]

However, even though a privilege was to be strictly interpreted, it had to be interpreted in such a way that it actually conferred something, and was not rendered useless.[42]

[35] Reiffenstuel, Lib. I, tit. II, n. 45; Schmalzgrueber, Lib. I, tit. III, nn. 29-31.

[36] Barbosa, *Tractatus varii, Axiomata,* Axioma 222, n. 4; Reiffenstuel, Lib. I, tit. III, nn. 29-31.

[37] C. 18, X, *de rescriptis,* I, 3.

[38] *Loc. cit.*

[39] *Ius Ecclesiasticum Universum,* Lib. I, tit. III, nn. 24-26.

[40] Schmalzgrueber, *ibid.,* n. 28.

[41] See p. 34.

[42] C. 30, X, *de privilegiis et excessibus privilegiatorum,* V, 33: ". . . ita quod dicti Fratres aliquam ex nostra indulgentia in hoc gratiam consecuti."

Section 3. Rubrics, Summaries, and Glosses

Rubrics as added to the law by private individuals, as for example in the *Decretum Gratiani,* did not have any authentic force, since they were not authoritatively approved. However, rubrics which had received official approbation were authentic and could be of great assistance for a proper understanding and interpretation of the laws. The rubrics of the titles in the official collection of the Decretals were authentic, because they had been approved together with the laws.[43] Sometimes the relationship between the text of the law (*nigrum*) and the rubrics is quite complicated and difficult to understand, but some general points can be mentioned to show how the rubrics assisted in the interpreting of the law. Canonists cited the well known maxim, *"Bene valet argumentum a rubro ad nigrum."* [44]

Generally the rubrics did no more than apply in particular cases the general rules previously mentioned. Thus, if the words of a law could have two meanings, the meaning that more aptly agreed with the rubric was to be taken. Thus the *Glossa* to the decretal law *"Bonae memoriae"* shows that the case was that of confirming a simple sentence of the first instance, and not the case of an appeal, since this law was placed under the title *"De confirmatione,"* and not under the title *"De appellatione."* [45]

Again, when the words of the law were obscure or ambiguous, the rubrics could help to clarify the law. For example, the Glossator to the decretal law *"Cum monasterium"* interpreted

---

And the *Glossa* s. v. *Ex indulgentia:* "Indulgentia enim semper debet aliquid conferre: ut hic patet . . . et potius laborandum est, ut res valeat, quam pereat . . . alias delusoria esset indulgentia principis."

[43] Consult the *Prooemium* to the Decretals of Gregory IX and of Boniface VIII. Also the *Glossa* s. v. *Titulus,* Prooemium in VI°: "Nota rubricas esse authenticas." Panormitanus stated: "Item collige rubricas esse authenticas."—*Commentaria, Prooemium, Rex pacificus,* n. 2.

[44] "Hoc est a rubrica ad textum canonis seu legis."—Reiffenstuel, Lib. I, tit. II, n. 96.

[45] *Glossa* s. v. *Tamdiu,* ad c. 3, X, *de confirmatione utili vel inutili,* II, 30: ". . . et ista fuit simplex confirmatio . . . alias quare fuisset haec decretalis in titulo isto? Potius debuisset poni in titulo de appellatione."

the word *"postulatio"* to mean *"electio,"* and one of the reasons given for this interpretation was the fact that this chapter of law was placed under the title *"De electione,"* and not under the preceding title *"De postulatione."*[46]

Because of the rubrics the law could sometimes be extended beyond the actual words of the law, and in this case, if the rubric was clear and consisted of a complete sentence, and was not just a general phrase or a heading which in its import was more general than the words of the law, the law could be extended in consequence of the rubric.[47]

But if the law was more general than the rubric, it was not restricted by the rubric.[48] However, such an extension could not be made if it was contrary to custom, to practice, or to the procedure of the legislator, or if such an extension contradicted the text of the law.[49]

The inscriptions in the Decretals were authentic, since the whole body of laws had been approved successively by Gregory IX and Boniface VIII. Their value was similar to that of the rubrics in the interpretation of the laws contained therein.[50]

Summaries of the laws of the Decretals were composed and inserted by private individuals and therefore had no authentic force, but they had great doctrinal merit and assisted in the gaining of an understanding of the laws.[51]

Finally, the Glosses to the Decretals were also composed by doctors, and remained without legislative force. They had no authentic force as law, but because of the authority of the Glossators they possessed considerable doctrinal value.[52]

[46] *Glossa* s. v. *Postulantes,* ad c. 13, X, *de electione et electi potestate,* I, 6.

[47] "Si rubrica generalior nigro habet orationem perfectam, debet attendi . . . licet in nigro non sit mentio generalis, sed stricta."—Tuschus, *Practicae Conclusiones,* VII, Litt. R, concl. 370, n. 2.

[48] Tuschus, *ibid.,* n. 26.

[49] Tuschus, *ibid.,* n. 18.

[50] Schmalzgrueber, *op. cit.,* Dissert. Prooem, n. 303.

[51] Schmalzgrueber, *ibid.,* n. 302.

[52] See p. 17.

Article III. Prohibitions of Doctrinal Interpretation in Canon Law

It was noted early in the study that doctrinal interpretation is necessary in almost all human laws. Nevertheless from time to time, for various good reasons, doctrinal interpretation has been forbidden in canon law.

The decretal law *"Exiit"* repeated a constitution of Nicholas III (1277-1280), which contained a clause forbidding interpretation of the constitution itself, except in the very narrowest sense of the term. It allowed a literal exposition of it, but it did not allow any other kind of gloss. From this prohibition it can be concluded that no argument from the mind of the legislator, no restriction or extension of the meaning of the words, nor any other principles of doctrinal interpretation were allowed. Therefore it permitted only an exposition of the proper signification of the words in text and context.[53]

Pius IV (1559-1565) in the Bull *"Benedictus Deus,"* by which he confirmed the Council of Trent, prohibited any commentaries on the decrees of this Council to be printed, in order to prevent all perversion and confusion in the laws. Any interpretation of doubts or of uncertainties arising from these laws was to be done by the Apostolic See.[54] But it does not seem that Pius IV meant to prohibit an exposition of the decrees of the Council in the schools, that is, privately, for in this Bull he

[53] "Exiit," 14 aug. 1297—Potthast, *Regesta Pontificum Romanorum inde ab Anno post Christum Natum 1198 ad Annum 1304* (Berolini, 1874-1875), n. 21628; C. 3, *de verborum significatione,* V, 12, in VI°.

[54] *Benedictus Deus,* 26 ian. 1564: "Ad vitandum praeterea perversionem, et confusionem, quae oriri possent, si unicuique liceret . . . in decreta concilii commentarios et interpretationes suas edere . . . (Prohibemus) ne quis, sine auctoritate nostra, audeat ullos commentarios, glossas, annotationes, scholia, ullumve omnino interpretationis genus super ipsius Concilii decretis quocumque modo edere, aut quidquam quocumque nomine, etiam sub praetextu maioris decretorum corroborationis, aut executionis, aliove quaesito colore, statuere."—*Magnum Bullarium Romanum* (a Beato Leone Magno (440-461) usque ad S. D. N. Benedictum XIV (1740-1758), Editio Novissima, 8 vols., Luxemburgi, 1727), VII, 245-246.

mentioned only the editing of commentaries and glosses as prohibited.[55]

Tuschus was of the opinion that if a statute forbade interpretation and glosses, and commanded an exact observance of the words of the statute, nevertheless some interpretation could be admitted, for example, an interpretation which proceeded from the common manner of speaking, especially if this was not contrary to the proper signification of the statute. He also held that interpretation was allowed if the words were ambiguous and had several meanings; however, all frivolous interpretation was forbidden.[56]

[55] Schmalzgrueber, Lib. I, tit. II, n. 46.

[56] *Practicae Conclusiones,* IV, Litt. I, concl. 333, nn. 1-8.

PART II

CANONICAL COMMENTARY

CHAPTER V

INTERPRETATION IN THE CODE OF CANON LAW

Article I. Definition of Interpretation

In the Code of Canon Law, the words *interpres* and *interpretatio* are used in different senses. Thus an *interpreter* designates one who translates an unknown language into one that is known. Mention is made of an interpreter in confession,[1] in matrimony,[2] and in trials.[3] Interpretation, on the other hand, signifies the explanation and declaration of a certain thing, and in this sense the Code speaks of the interpretation of laws,[4] rescripts,[5] privileges,[6] oaths,[7] punishments,[8] and the reservation of censures.[9] The Code, however, does not give an official definition of interpretation, though in canon 18 it sets forth the fundamental rules for the doctrinal interpretation of law. The subject matter of this study is limited to a treatment of the doctrinal interpretation of law, and therefore it does not include the interpretation of rescripts, of privileges or of contracts, though the rules for the interpretation of these are in many respects similar.

Interpretation of law supposes first of all the existence of laws, and, secondly, laws which are doubtful or obscure. This is readily understood, for if a law does not exist it cannot be explained,[10] and if the law is already clear there is no need for

[1] Canons 889, § 2, and 903.

[2] Canon 1090.

[3] Canons 1641 and 2073, § 3.

[4] Canons 17, 18, 19, 29.

[5] Canon 50.

[6] Canon 68.

[7] Canon 1321.

[8] Canon 2219.

[9] Canon 2246, § 2.

[10] The term interpretation is frequently used in an improper sense to denote the application of the provisions of law regarding a certain matter to another matter about which there is no law. This is not *interpretation*

interpretation: "*Cum in verbis nulla ambiguitas est, non debet admitti voluntatis quaestio.*"[11] In its ultimate effect interpretation removes all doubt and obscurity, so that the law becomes clear and certain. Before interpretation the law is doubtful and obscure, but later, through interpretation, it is freed of doubt and ambiguity and becomes clear and defined. However, it is still the same law which before had remained obscure and afterwards was rendered clear. Thus interpretation does not in any way affect the essence of the law, which remains the same before and after.[12]

In defining the word *interpretation* some authors seem to place a greater emphasis on the words of the law, while others stress the importance of the mind of the legislator. Interpretation is usually defined in one of two ways:

a) For some, interpretation is the explanation of the sense of the law according to the mind of the legislator.[13]

b) For others, interpretation is the explanation of the sense of the law according to the words of the law.[14]

---

of law in the proper sense of the word, but its *supplementation*. This situation is considered in canon 20. Again the use of *epikeia* (a benign interpretation exempting one from the law in a way that proves contrary to the clear words of the law but in accordance with the mind of the legislator) is at times, though improperly, called interpretation.

11 D. (32, 1) 25. If all laws were perfectly clear and obvious there would be no need for canon 18.

12 Fagnanus, *Commentaria super Quinque Libros Decretalium,* Lib. I, tit. 3, cap. Quoniam, n. 14: "Quemadmodum cum nucleus ex nuce, et grana ex spicis eruuntur, speciem non mutant, sed sunt idem nucleus et eadem grana, ita et declaratio, cum ex visceribus legis educitur, nihil aliud est quam ipsa lex."

13 Philippus Maroto, *Institutiones Iuris Canonici* (2 vols., Romae, 1919-1921), I, 246; Mattheus Conte a Coronata, *Institutiones Iuris Canonici* (5 vols., Vols. I, II, 2. ed., Taurini: Ex Officina Marietti, 1939), I, 36.

14 A. Brems, "De Interpretatione Authentica Codicis.—I.C. per Pont. Commissionem," *Jus Pontificium,* XV (1935), 178-179; F. X. Wernz, *Ius Decretalium* (6 vols., Romae, 1898-1914; Vol. I, 2. ed., 1905), I, 127; A. Van Hove, *Commentarium Lovaniense in Codicem Iuris Canonici* (1 Tom. in 5 vols., Vol. II, *De Legibus Ecclesiasticis,* Mechliniae: H. Dessain, 1930), II, 247; Gommarus Michiels, *Normae Generales Iuris Canonici* (2. ed., 2 vols., Parisiis-Tornaci-Romae: Typis societatis S. Joannis Evangelistae,

Although these two definitions seem, at a glance, to be quite similar, they are really quite different. According to the first definition the ultimate objective in interpretation is the disclosure of the mind of the legislator as manifested in the words of the law. According to the second definition, on the other hand, the main objective is the disclosure of the meaning of the words of the law. Therefore, if one accepts the first definition, one's chief occupation will be to answer the question: What does the legislator mean by these words? Whereas, if one prefers the second definition, one's task will be to answer the question: What do these words mean?

The first definition is based on the presumption that the words of the law may not always objectively correspond precisely to the mind of the legislator, and consequently there may be a difference between the meaning of the words of the law and the idea existing in the mind of the legislator. Therefore the real task of interpretation is the disclosure of the mind of the legislator, manifested, of course, in some way in the law.[15] The second definition is based on the presumption that the words of the law exactly correspond to the mind of the legislator, so that there can be no difference between the meaning of the words of the law and the idea existing in the mind of the legislator. All that is necessary is to disclose the meaning of the words.[16]

In the comparing of these two definitions, these observations should be made. There can be a difference between the words of the law taken in their proper signification, on the one hand, and the mind of the legislator, on the other. Sometimes the words

---

Desclée et Socii, 1949), I, 471; Felix Cappello, *Summa Iuris canonici* (3 vols., Vol. I, 4. ed., Romae: Apud Aedes Universitatis Gregorianae, 1945), I, n. 84. The foregoing define interpretation as the explanation of the sense contained in the law. Cf. also Cicognani, *Canon Law* (2. ed., The Newman Press, Westminster, Maryland: Reprint, 1949), p. 598, who defines interpretation as a declaration or explanation of the true meaning of the law.

15 "Codex . . . in can. 18 et 19 indicat normas sequendas ut mens legislatoris detegatur. Huius suprema regula est voluntas legislatoris, aliquo modo saltem in formula legis expressa."—Van Hove, *De Legibus Ecclesiasticis,* p. 250.

16 "Discrimen inter interpretationem juxta verba legis et interpretationem juxta mentem legislatoris non est admittendum."—Brems, "art. cit.," *loc. cit.*

are ambiguous and they do not always clearly express what the legislator has in mind; at other times the words are clear in themselves, but they do not exactly and factually express the mind of the legislator, either because they overstate or understate what is actually in his mind. That this difference can, and often does, exist is evident from the whole idea of interpretation, since all interpretation presupposes that the words, in a particular instance, do not clearly and exactly represent to the subject what the legislator has in mind.[17]

It is to be noted that such a difference, as a general rule, does not frequently exist, since the legislator chooses the words of the law with great care, and these will ordinarily express his mind faithfully. Thus the presumption is warranted that the words faithfully represent the mind of the legislator. But presumption must always cede to fact.[18] This difference must be admitted juridically,[19] and the interpreter who does not admit this difference and interprets accordingly violates the axiom: "It is certain that he violates the law who follows the word of the law and not the will of the law."[20] Though authors unanimously agree that the best and most secure means of discovering the mind of the legislator is to be sought through the words of the law, nevertheless they do not hesitate to affirm that other means of interpretation may at times prove that the mind of the

[17] "Verba clara non admittunt interpretationem, neque voluntatis coniecturam. Ubi sunt verba clara non relinquatur locus interpretationis."—Card. Tuschus, *Practicae Conclusiones,* VIII, Litt. V. concl. 110; Barbosa, *Tractatus Varii, Axiomata,* Axioma 202.

[18] "Scire leges non hoc est verba tenere, sed vim et potestatem."—D. (1, 3) 17;"Recedimus a verbis propter mentem."—Card. Tuschus, *Practicae Conclusiones,* VIII, Litt. V, concl. 79, n. 10; "Interpretatio potius menti quam verbis convenire debet."—Reiffenstuel, Lib. I, tit. II, n. 386.

[19] "At etsi maxime verba legis hanc significationem habent, tamen sententia legislatoris aliud flagitat."—D. (27. 1) (13. 2).

[20] Reg. 88, R. J., in VI°. ". . . Rogo non verbum ex verbo sed sensum ex sensu transferri: quia plerumque, dum propriatas verborum attenditur, sensus veritatis amittitur."—C. 8, x, *de verborum significatione,* V. 40; "Mens enim magis quam verborum sonus est attendenda discrete."—Eugenius IV, ep. *Fide digna,* 8 iul. 1440—*Fontes,* n. 53.

legislator may be different from what the words of the law indicate.[21]

Every law, adequately considered, is composed of two elements: the mind or will of the legislator (*mens*), and the words of the law (*verba*).[22] The mind or will of the legislator is the intrinsic form of the law.[23] Therefore the mind or will of the legislator constitutes or determines the subject matter of the law, and the words manifest this subject matter to the subjects of the law. The words of the law are the principal source indicative of the mind of the legislator, but they are not the only source. In conjunction with these, there are other norms of interpretation, e.g., parallel passages, the purpose of the law, circumstances, etc. Since the mind of the legislator determines the subject matter of the law, the purpose of interpretation is the discovery of the mind of the legislator. The best way of discovering the mind of the legislator is that of weighing the words of his law. When the words of the law present no difficulty, one cannot use any other means. But when the words of the legislator present a difficulty, one must employ other means also, such as the purpose of the law, circumstances, etc.

From the foregoing the following conclusions can be drawn:

1) The end of interpretation is the disclosure of the mind of the legislator.[24]

2) The principal means to this end is the careful weighing and appraising of the words of the law. That the end of interpretation is the disclosure of the mind of the legislator and not that of the words of the law is confirmed implicitly in canon 18. For if the end of interpretation were the disclosure of the meaning of the words of the law, then the legislator would not have indicated a subsidiary means of interpretation such considerations as parallel passages, the purpose of the law, the circumstances, and the mind of the legislator.

[21] See notes 18-19-20, above; Michiels, *Normae Generales Iuris Canonici*, I, 474; Van Hove, *De Legibus Ecclesiasticis*, p. 250.

[22] D. (1, 3) 17; cc. 6, 8, X, *de verborum significatione*, V, 40.

[23] Suarez, *De Legibus*, Lib. VI, cap. I, n. 15.

[24] "Illa est ergo vera interpretatio legis per quam mentem et voluntatem legislatoris assequimur."—Suarez, *De Legibus*, Lib. VI, cap. 1, n. 12.

ARTICLE II. DIVISIONS OF INTERPRETATION

Upon this consideration of the notion of interpretation, it may be opportune, for the sake of clarity, to distinguish the different types of interpretation properly so called. The general division given by most authors is threefold, according to the source or authorship, according to effect, and according to mode or method.[25]

a) According to authorship or the source from which it originates, interpretation is authoritative, usual and doctrinal. It is *authoritative* or *authentic,* if it is given by the lawmaker himself, his successor, or one to whom the power of interpretation has been delegated. Authoritative interpretation is *general,* if it is given in the form of law; it is *particular,* when it is given in the form of a judicial sentence, or of a particular rescript.[26] Interpretation is *doctrinal,* when it is given by private persons skilled in canon law. It is usual or customary, when it is derived from custom.[27]

b) According to its effect, interpretation is purely declarative, comprehensive, extensive and restrictive. It is *purely declarative* when it explains terms of the law which are in themselves clear.[28] It is *comprehensive* if it explains a doubtful or obscure

[25] Cappello, *Summa Iuris Canonici,* I, n. 84; Cicognani, *Canon Law,* p. 598; Maroto, *Institutiones Iuris Canonici,* I, n. 236. The division according to *origin* or *source* is found frequently; cf. Suarez, *De Legibus,* Lib. VI, cap. I, n. 1; Reiffenstuel, *Ius Canonicum Universum,* Lib. I, tit. II, n. 357; Schmalzgrueber, *Ius Ecclesiasticum Universum,* Lib. I, tit. II, n. 44. The division according to *effect* is also found in Suarez, *De Legibus,* Lib. VI, cap. II, n. 1; Reiffenstuel, Lib. I, tit. II, n. 365. The division according to *method* is found in the more recent authors; cf. Van Hove, *De Legibus Ecclesiasticis,* p. 251; Cicognani, *Canon Law,* p. 599.

[26] Canon 17, §§ 2-3.

[27] "Immo magnae autoritatis hoc ius habetur, quod in tantum probatum est, ut non fuerit necesse scripto id comprehendere."—D. (1, 3) 36.

[28] Nicholas III, in his constitution *Exiit, qui seminat,* inserted a paragraph permitting the declaration of this constitution, but forbidding any other type of interpretation. ". . . Districte praecipmus, ut praesens constitutio, cum ipsam legi contigerit, sicut prolata est, sic fideliter exponatur ad litteram, concordantiae contrarietates, seu diversae vel adversae opiniones a lectoribus seu expositoribus nullatenus inducantur. Supra ipsa constitutione glossa non fiant, nisi forsan, per quas verbum vel verbi sensus, seu

law. It is *extensive* when it is extended to cases not comprised in the terms of the law. It is *restrictive* if it limits or curtails the sense of the law.[29]

c) According to the method in which it is made, interpretation is grammatical or literal, logical, historic and systematic. It is *grammatical* or literal, when it declares the meaning of terms, analyzing the text and context in the light of common or juridic usage. This type of interpretation is used mostly in the declaration of clear laws in which the interpreter has only to analyze the terms of the law and give the proper value to each part of the legal formula. Interpretation is *logical* when in consequence of the obscurity or doubtfulness of the words of the law other principles of interpretation must be used, that is, it goes beyond the words of the law to disclose the mind of the legislator. The interpreter investigates the mind and intention of the legislator by means which, though extrinsic to the law, are nevertheless more or less intimately connected with the law. Thus he may examine the preparatory drafts and discussions which preceded the making of the law, considering also the general principles of justice and utility which, as he presumes, guided the legislator in his making of the law. Interpretation is *historic,* when it considers the state of law and fact which existed at the time of the promulgation of the law, or interprets the new law in the light of the old, since law is not formed by one act, but develops over a period of time. Interpretation is *systematic,*

---

constructio, vel ipsa constructio, quasi grammaticaliter ad letteram vel intelligibilius exponatur."—C. 3, *de verborum significatione,* V, 12, in VI°, *in fine.*

[29] There is a great deal of difference among authors in their definitions of comprehensive, extensive and restrictive interpretation. The older authors often used the term *comprehensive* to denote any interpretation which was *ad mentem legislatoris,* even though it might be extensive in the sense of the words. Cf. Suarez, *De Legibus,* Lib. VI, cap. III, n. 9; Reiffenstuel, Lib. I, tit. II, n. 372; Schmalzgrueber, Lib. I, tit. II, n. 44. They again differ in their definition of *extensive* and *restrictive* interpretation. Some consider interpretation extensive or restrictive according as it extends or restricts the mind of the legislator. Cf. Maroto, *Institutiones Iuris Canonici,* 1, 247. Others consider interpretation extensive or restrictive according as it extends or restricts the sense of the words of the law. Cf. Conte a Coronata, *Institutiones Iuris Canonici,* I, n. 22.

when it discloses the meaning of the law through a study of the entire juridic system, since for a thorough understanding of the mind of the legislator one must see the position and the action of the law in the general legal system. Each law must be considered as a part of the whole. This is true especially in codified law. A particular law must be considered in relation to all the other laws with which it forms a complete unit. Thus, when several laws are considered, it may seem at first sight that one contradicts the other, but a further study of the entire structure may reveal that the law in question is perhaps considering another case, or placing an exception to the general law, or completing another law.[30]

From this description according to method it is readily understood that this division is not properly a division of interpretation, but rather an enumeration of the different means or aids of interpretation. It is a division of method rather than of interpretation. These four elements (grammatical, logical, historical and systematic) do not form four species of interpretation in the sense that one may be selected to the exclusion of the others, but four intellectual operations that should all concur for the interpretation of law, although in a particular instance one or the other may have greater importance.[31]

[30] Van Hove, *De Legibus Ecclesiasticis*, p. 258; Michiels, *Normae Generales Iuris Canonici*, I, 482; Maroto, *op. cit.*, I, 249; Cicognani, *Canon Law*, p. 599.

[31] F. C. Savigny, *Sistema del diritto romano attuale*, Vol. I (Traduzione dall'originale tedesco di Vittorio Scialoja, Torino, 1886), p. 222.

CHAPTER VI

THE PRIMARY RULE FOR DOCTRINAL INTERPRETATION

Leges ecclesiasticae intelligendae sunt secundum propriam verborum significationem in textu et contextu consideratam. . . . Ecclesiastical laws must be understood according to the proper meaning of the words of the law considered in their text and context.

ARTICLE I. LEGES ECCLESIASTICAE

The subject matter of interpretation in canon 18 is *ecclesiastical* laws. It may seem quite superfluous to remark here that only *ecclesiastical* laws are meant, since it is presumed that this is already understood. Nevertheless the legislator considered it useful and quite necessary to emphasize the fact that he is prescinding from the method observed in any other kind of legislation.[1] He also excluded the interpretation of the eternal law and the divine law, both natural and positive, since these pertain to the studies of philosophy and theology. Again, ecclesiastical laws, in so far as they pertain to the internal forum, are part of moral theology.[2] It is also necessary to note that this canon does not apply to the interpretation of rescripts, of privileges and of contracts. Though the rules for interpreting these subject matters are in many respects common and similar, they are in other respects peculiar and dissimilar.[3]

[1] Cicognani, *Canon Law,* p. 608.

[2] Van Hove, *De Legibus Ecclesiasticis,* p. 81. Although the Code contains many laws which refer to the natural and positive divine law, it is not the official interpreter of these. They are interpreted by the science to which they pertain: ". . . ut Codex eas tantumodo leges complecteretur, quae disciplinam spectant. Nihil tamen prohibeat, quominus in Codice principia quaedam attingi possent aut deberent, quae ad ius naturae vel ad ipsam Fidem referrentur." Preface to the Code. See also Michiels, *Normae Generales Iuris Canonici,* I, 207-211.

[3] A. Brems, "De Interpretatione Authentica Codicis I. C. per Pont. Commissionem," *Jus Pontificium,* XV (1935), 164.

Since no other limitation is added, the legislator wishes to include *all* ecclesiastical laws, not only those which are contained in the Code, but also those which have been enacted since the promulgation of the Code or will be in the future. Therefore, whether the laws be universal or particular, general or special, favorable, odious or penal, diocesan statutes or any particular body of ecclesiastical law, they are to be interpreted according to the norms contained in canon 18.[4]

However a very far-reaching restriction is placed on canon 18 by canon 6, nn. 2, 3, 4 and 6, the provisions of which will be dealt with in the following numbers.

1. *Canones qui ius vetus ex integro referunt, ex veteris iuris auctoritate, atque ideo ex receptis apud probatos auctores interpretationibus, sunt aestimandi.*[5]

The canons which re-state the former laws in their entirety must be interpreted upon the authority of the old law, and therefore according to the interpretation already given by approved authors.

By the "old law" the Code means all previous legislation, and it commands that those canons which re-state the old legislation without change must be interpreted upon the authority of the old law. In this case the interpretative authority under the old law does not cease, but continues in force, and recourse must be had to it.[6] However, the present laws, be they old or new, receive their binding force not from the old discipline but from

[4] Van Hove, *op. cit.*, p. 81.

[5] Canon 6, n. 2.

[6] "When the legislator speaks of the *auctoritas* in antecedent legislation, he refers to its evaluation and intrinsic worth. It is the sum and substance which the mind of the legislator reveals. The juridical terminology, the object, the adjuncts, and the context of the law all manifest the mind of the legislator. In addition to these requisites the word *auctoritas* includes the interpretations of the old legislation, for this is another form of disclosing the legislator's mind."—Nicholas J. Neuberger, *Canon 6, or the Relation of the Codex Iuris Canonici to Preceding Legislation,* The Catholic University of America Canon Law Studies, n. 44 (Washington, D. C.: The Catholic University of America, 1927), p. 71 (hereafter cited Neuberger). The *auctoritas* also includes the authentic, customary and doctrinal interpretations of the old law. Cf. Michiels, *Normae Generales Iuris Canonici,* I, 142.

the Code itself, since the direct and exclusive font of the present law is the new Code, and not the old law.[7]

Nowhere does the law define just who are the approved authors. Canon Law has never recognized a jurist who has been given the "*ius respondendi.*" It has, however, held the interpretative authority of the doctors in high repute, especially when they are in agreement on the interpretation of laws. Certainly the Code here refers to the *probati auctores* who have written before the Code and includes, in general, jurists from Gratian down to the time of the Code who were outstanding canonists and devoted to Catholic Doctrine. In particular, though there is no official list of approved canonists, those who are frequently used and quoted by the Roman Curia are without doubt to be considered among the principal authorities. However, from this list are not to be excluded authors who are generally recognized by other experts as outstanding, even though they have not been regularly cited by the Roman Curia.[8]

2. *Canones qui ex parte tantum cum veteri iure congruunt, ex iure antiquo aestimandi sunt; qua discrepant, sunt ex sua ipsorum sententia diiudicandi.*[9]

Those canons which agree only in part with the old law must be interpreted according to the old law in the part in which they agree with it; in the parts in which they differ from it, they must be interpreted according to the meaning of the words employed.

In the preface to the Code Cardinal Gasparri wrote: "*Vix animadvertere attinet, canones haud semper cum suis fontibus omni ex parte in sententia congruere.*" Canons abound in which the old law is partially embodied while a new prescription supplants that part of the old law which has been derogated. It was the purpose of the legislator to rejuvenate what was useful

[7] Neuberger, p. 71; Van Hove, *De Legibus Ecclesiasticis,* p. 67; Cicognani, *Canon Law,* p. 502. It may be added here as a logical consequence that authentic interpretations given in the old law and contained explicitly or implicitly in the new law receive their binding force from the new law.

[8] Michiels, *Normae Generales Iuris Canonici,* I, 144-145; Van Hove, *De Legibus Ecclesiasticis,* pp. 69-70. For a list of approved authors cf. any authority who has written on the history of Canon Law, e.g., Cicognani, *Canon Law;* A. Van Hove, *Prolegomena;* see also Neuberger, pp. 75-78.

[9] Canon 6, n. 3.

in the old law and to discard the obsolete and the useless. "*Quia utile per inutile non debet vitiari.*"[10] Where such a conflict exists, the legislator has supplied rules of interpretation. Whenever the canons agree with the old enactments the old law is the interpreter; whenever a discrepancy exists, those parts of the new law which differ from the old law must be interpreted *ex sua ipsorum sententia,* that is, they are to be interpreted in a sense proper to themselves, according to the rules of interpretation given in canons 18 and 19.[11]

In dubio num aliquod canonum praescriptum cum veteri iure discrepet, a veteri iure non est recedendum.[12]

In doubt the presumption is in favor of the former legislation. Therefore it must be proved that the canon differs from the old law. Often the words themselves will immediately indicate that they have been taken from the old law, however the canon as a whole must be examined and inspected. If a positive doubt exists, that is, when there is a well founded reason for affirming now, and again denying, no departure is to be made from the old law.[13] In order to depart from the old law one must be morally certain that the law which one is now examining is not contained in the former discipline.[14]

Si qua ex ceteris disciplinaribus legibus, quae usque adhuc viguerunt, nec explicite nec implicite in Codice contineatur, ea vim omnem amisisse dicenda est.[15]

Former laws which are explicitly or implicitly contained in the Code must therefore be interpreted upon the authority of the old law, and according to the interpretations already given by the old authors. Authors do not agree on the definitions of *explicite*

[10] Neuberger, p. 79.

[11] Neuberger, p. 81; Van Hove, *De Legibus Ecclesiasticis,* p. 68; Cicognani, *Canon Law,* p. 503.

[12] Canon 6, n. 4.

[13] Michiels, *op. cit.,* I, 145; Cicognani, *op. cit.,* p. 503.

[14] Van Hove, *op. cit.,* p. 69.

[15] All other disciplinary laws of the old law which were in force until now, if they are neither explicitly nor implicitly contained in the Code, have lost all force of law.

and *implicite.*[16] An acceptable definition of laws implicitly contained in the Code was given by Noval (1861-1938).[17]

Some canons have prescriptions which are evidently incomplete. An instance is seen in canon 99. *"In Ecclesia, praeter personas physicas, sunt etiam personae morales, publica auctoritate constitutae, quae distinguuntur in personas morales collegiales et non collegiales, ut ecclesiae, Seminaria, beneficia, etc.,"* The *"etc."* makes allowance for other examples not mentioned in the canon. Again there are many prescriptions which are not classified *"taxative."* Such are introduced with the word *"praesertim"*; *"hae causae sunt praesertim"*;[18] *"poenae vindictivae . . . praesertim sunt,"*[19] *"praecipuae poenitentiae sunt praecepta."*[20]

It is generally agreed that the following are found explicitly in the Code:

a) Antecedent laws which are transferred verbatim into the Code. Thus, canon 866, § 1: *"Omnibus fidelibus cuiusvis ritus datur facultas ut, pietatis causa, sacramentum Eucharisticum quolibet ritu confectum suscipiant,"* is a restatement of the Apostolic Constitution *"Tradita ab antiquis."*[21]

b) Legislation converted into canons not in the identical but in equivalent terms. Most of the previous enactments adopted from previous legislators are thus contained in the Code. Thus canon 2149, § 2, reconstructs with the same meaning a prescription of the Decree *"Maxima cura."*[22]

[16] Cf. Michaels, *ibid.*, pp. 132-136; A. Vermeersch–J. Creusen, *Epitome Iuris Canonici* (3 vols., Vol. I, 7. ed., Mechliniae-Romae: H. Dessain, 1949), I, 77: Cicognani, *op. cit.*, p. 507; Van Hove, *op. cit.*, pp. 73-74.

[17] Josephus Noval, *Codificationis Juris Canonici Recensio Historico-Apologetica et Codicis Piano-Benedictini Notitia Generalis* (Romae, 1918), p. 47: *"Quae ex eo (Codice) deducuntur directe quia in lege ibidem expressa includuntur, tamquam conclusio in principio, vel species in genere, vel pars in toto, vel id quod minus in eo quod maius est."*

[18] Canon 2147, § 2.

[19] Canon 2291.

[20] Canon 2313, § 1.

[21] *Acta Apostolici Sedis (AAS), Commentarium officiale* (Romae, 1909-), IV (1912), hereafter cited *AAS*).

[22] *AAS*, II (1910), 636.

Some Apostolic Constitutions are not transcribed into canons. The substance of these canons, however, is found in the particular Constitutions from which they are derived or to which the canons refer. These are equivalent to laws transcribed into the Code. Such legislation usually reads, "*Ad normam constitutionum Apostolicarum.*"[23] These three classes actually exist in the Code and such laws are explicitly contained in the new legislation.[24] Vermeersch-Creusen define laws implicitly contained in the Code as, "leges antiquiores quarum praescripta ex textu canonum via *necessariae* consecutionis permanere constat, tamquam applicationem certam principii in Codice contenti; et praeterea leges sine quibus canon vel series canonum nullo modo intelligi vel applicari posset."[25]

From the foregoing brief consideration of canon 6, one readily understands that it would be a grave error to attempt to interpret all laws exclusively according to the norms contained in canon 18 of the Code, for the norms of canon 6 must also be considered. One must understand the relationship existing between the Code and the old law, and use the old law as a means of interpreting the new. From this it follows that in order to correctly interpret the new law and the juridical institutes and prescriptions contained therein, it is necessary not only to know the new law, but one must also be well versed in the old. One must know whether the concrete matter with which one is dealing in the new law existed before in some prescript of the old, whether the old law is certainly or doubtfully opposed to the new (for in the first case the new law prevails, in the second the old), and, finally, if the old law corresponds to the new, what interpretation was given by the old authors.[26]

Article II. Intelligendae Sunt

The literal translation of these words is, "must be understood." The legislator used the gerundive to indicate that this is more

[23] Canons 904 and 884.

[24] Vermeersch-Creusen, *Epitome Iuris Canonici,* I, 77-78; Van Hove, *De Legibus Ecclesiasticis,* p. 73; Michiels, *Normae Generales Iuris Canonici,* I, 133.

[25] Vermeersch-Creusen, *loc. cit.*

[26] Michiels, *ibid.,* pp. 146-147; Noval, *op. cit.,* pp. 60-61.

than a directive or suggestion; it is a command, and the interpreter is warned that he is bound by the law itself to use the means contained therein when he applies himself to the task of interpretation.

ARTICLE III. SECUNDUM PROPRIAM VERBORUM SIGNIFICATIONEM

Since a law is essentially a determined act of the will of the legislator manifested in a determined way, namely, defined and circumscribed by a verbal formula, and since precisely with this specific formula, and not otherwise, does he intend to express his will, this verbal formula alone authentically contains and apodictically manifests the will of the legislator. From this premise it follows that to interpret a law is nothing else than to inquire into and determine the whole and sole will of the legislator as it is expressed in this verbal formula, or to search out and manifest the true sense of the words as they are employed by the legislator, subtracting nothing which is really contained in the words and adding nothing to the true meaning of the words; neither more, nor less, nor something different from what has been signified by the words, but only what is signified.[27] *"Quorsum enim sunt verba nisi ut demonstrarent voluntatem dicentis?"* [28]

In every human law, first of all, the proper meaning of the words is to be considered, for from the words is discovered the true interpretation of the law. This means must always be preferred unless something stands in the way.[29]

The reason is evident. If in ordinary speech words are used according to their proper meaning, there is much greater reason to so employ them in the formulation of laws, since laws must be clear and not exposed to circumvention and false interpretation. Otherwise nothing would be certain in laws nor could they regulate the actions of men, since everyone could interpret them in their improper sense according to his own whim.[30] *"Quod*

[27] Michiels, *ibid.*, pp. 472-473.

[28] Michiels, *ibid.*, p. 473.

[29] Suarez, *De Legibus*, Lib. VI, cap. I, n. 6; Schmalzgrueber, *Ius Ecclesiasticum Universum*, Lib. I, tit. II, n. 47.

[30] Suarez, *De Legibus*, Lib. VI, cap. I, n. 8.

voluit expressit, quod noluit tacuit, ideoque in dubio melius est verbis edicti servire." [31]

Most canonists offer a threefold distinction with reference to the concept of proper signification: natural, usual and juridical or canonical.[32]

The *natural* sense of the word arises from the original application of a name to a certain thing. Thus the word "*mors*" is understood in the sense of a natural death, and not of a juridic death; "*familia*" is understood to mean a natural family, not a religious family.[33]

The proper *usual* sense (*sensus usualis*) is the natural sense confirmed or changed through use or custom. The meaning of words is determined by the customary use that men make of them, and therefore the usual meaning or customary meaning may be called proper in the true sense of the word. The usual meaning of a word is learned from dictionaries and writings existing at the time that the law was made. Etymological or philosophical meanings of words are not considered except as an aid for the discovering of the proper meaning.[34]

The proper usual meaning of a word is that which it possessed at the time of the promulgation of the law, unless that meaning has been changed by custom or by the *stylus curiae*.[35] For it may happen that common usage has changed the original meaning of a word and has substituted a figurative meaning. In this case the figurative meaning has become the common one and must be accepted as such.[36] Or, again, it may happen that the custom or the usage in one region may have changed the ordinary signification of a word and attached to it another meaning.

[31] D. (14. 1) 20.

[32] Suarez, *De Legibus,* Lib. VI, cap. I, n. 9; Reiffenstuel, *Ius Canonicum Universum,* Lib. I, tit. II, n. 391; Michiels, *ibid.,* p. 259; Vermeersch-Creusen, *Epitome Iuris Canonici,* I, 123; Cicognani, *Canon Law,* p. 609.

[33] Van Hove, *op. cit.,* p. 260.

[34] Michiels, *ibid.,* p. 518; Van Hove, *op. cit.,* p. 261.

[35] Van Hove, *loc. cit.*

[36] D. (33, 10) (7, 2). *Glossa* s. v. *Ex communi usu:* "Scilicet, proprio aut figurato nam et figurativa significatio communis est et sic usitata potest appellari."

Then, as Bartolus noted, the custom of that region must be followed in the interpretation of its particular laws.[37]

The method of interpretation which discards the meaning which the word conveyed at the time of the promulgation of the law and substitutes another sense which perhaps is even more conducive to the common good is to be rejected. For the law is the expression of the will of the legislator, and he uses the words in accordance with the meaning which they possessed in his time.[38] Otherwise the judge or the interpreter is inducing his own law on his own authority. This is to be remembered when there is question of interpreting the old laws found in the Code, unless it is evident that the sense of the word has actually been changed by the Code itself or by custom. An example of this change is found in canon 707, in which confraternities are defined as "*Sodalitia in incrementum publici cultus erecta,*" for in the old law a confraternity was an "*associatio fidelium ad exercitium operis pietatis cuiuscumque.*"[39]

The proper *juridical* sense (*sensus iuridicus*) is that which has been determined by the use of jurists, or is determined by definition in the law itself, that is, the law defines the term or determines the meaning of it. The Code, unlike the old law, does not have a title "*de verborum significatione,*" but it frequently defines the juridical meaning of a word. Thus canon 7 defines what is meant by the terms *Sancta Sedis,* and *Romanus Pontifex;* canon 88 defines the words *puer, infans, minor;* and canon 488, *religio, ordo,* etc.[40] Canon 6 must not be forgotten here. Terminology which is clear from a new definition or from the accepted meaning needs no interpretation. When, however, the legislator has not defined a word in the Code, it is presumed that the traditional meaning established by the old definitions, by custom or by the common use of the jurists of the past, is intended.

[37] *Opera Omnia,* I, *Commentaria* in ff. *De Justitia et Jure,* 1. *Omnes populi* (D. [1, 1] 9), n. 58.

[38] François Geny, *Methode d'interpretation et sources en droit privé positif* (Paris, 1919), n. 99 (hereafter cited as Geny); Michiels, *ibid.,* p. 521; Cicognani, *Canon Law,* p. 609.

[39] Van Hove, *loc. cit.*

[40] Van Hove, *op. cit.,* p. 260.

Therefore, unless the contrary is established, the terms are to be accepted in the same sense as they were accepted in the old law.[41]

The juridical sense of words can also be determined from a comparison of the various texts in which they are used. But it must be noted that the Code is not consistent in its use of words. Consequently it is sometimes necessary to examine other sources in order to determine what the Code means when employing a certain word in a particular instance. Thus the word "*oportet*" in canons 765, 796 and 1459, § 2, is without doubt preceptive, whereas it is doubtful whether it is used in the sense of a command or only of a persuasion in canon 588, § 2.[42]

A word is used in the improper sense when the speaker substitutes a meaning other than the natural, usual or juridic, and supplies an arbitrary meaning. Thus, for example, he might use the word "*rogo*" in the sense of a command, whereas the proper meaning conveys simply the idea of a request.[43]

Article IV. In Textu et Contextu Consideratam

The text constitutes the original words of the author—the body of the matter on a printed page. Text is the same as a texture from the Latin word *textura*,[44] and it refers to the words of the legislator as situated each in its own particular place in the structure of the composition. Text may be defined as the combination of words which the legislator employs in expressing a particular prescript, with each word considered separately and

[41] Neuberger, pp. 81-82.

[42] Referring to the sacrament of baptism, canon 765 states: "*Ut quis sit patrinus oportet,*" and then it enumerates the required conditions. Canon 796 refers to the sacrament of confirmation in a like manner. Canon 1459 states that several independent patrons of one benefice may make an agreement to exercise the right of presentation in rotation, but in order that this agreement be valid, "*accedat oportet Ordinarii consensus in scriptis datis.*" Canon 588, § 2, states: "*Praefectus vel Magister spiritus iis qualitatibus praeditus sit oportet, quae in Magistro novitiorum requiruntur . . . .*" Cf. Van Hove, *op. cit.*, p. 261.

[43] Michiels, *ibid.*, p. 519.

[44] Albertus Toso, *Ad Codicem Iuris Canonici Commentaria Minora* (5 vols., Vols. I-II, Romae et Taurini: P. Marietti, 1920-1922), I, 57; Cicognani, *op. cit.*, p. 609.

singly in the sentence structure.[45] When doubt arises concerning the text of the law whether it be genuine or not, complete or incomplete, it is to be restored according to the rules of the art of criticism. In the Code of Canon Law it is scarcely necessary to consider this eventuality.[46]

The context is the arrangement of the words in a sentence or in a phrase—the connected structure of a writing. The words of the law should be considered not only singly and according to their written structure, but also conjointly, just as they are arranged in the proposition or sentence structure under consideration.[47] In order to discover the true meaning of a certain word as used in a certain verbal formula, the word is to be weighed not abstractly and separately, as if standing by itself and withdrawn from the formula in which it is used, but it is to be examined in the concrete, in conjunction with and dependent upon the other words used in the same formula. Very often the proper signification of some word in itself, or considered by itself alone, is general and somewhat indeterminate, but when considered in its relation to other words in the text and context it acquires a clear and concrete determination.[48] Thus, for example, the phrase "*matrimonium legitimum*" in canon 1015, § 3, means a valid matrimony between two non-baptized persons, while in canon 232, § 2, 2°, and in canon 1075, 1°, it denotes any legitimate wedlock; the word "*superior*" means one who has jurisdiction or dominative power, but in canon 564 it indicates only a religious superior whereas in canon 1383 it indicates a seminary rector.[49] Sometimes the text or context may make certain dictionary meanings of words or even their technical juridical meaning evidently inapplicable.[50]

A law consists, not in a mere material juxtaposition of concepts and words, but in a proposition or in a judgment derived

[45] Michiels, *loc. cit.*

[46] Sometimes mistakes may be found in certain editions of the Code. Cf. Van Hove, *De Legibus Ecclesiasticis,* p. 260.

[47] Cicognani, *op. cit.,* pp. 609-610.

[48] Michiels, *ibid.,* p. 522.

[49] Michiels, *loc. cit.*

[50] Bouscaren-Ellis, *Canon Law, A Text and Commentary* (Milwaukee: The Bruce Publishing Company, 1946), p. 33.

from these concepts. Hence, rather than insist on the sense of the individual words, one should attempt to discover the juridical principle derived from a consideration of all the words in the text and context, taken together and compared one with the other; then that interpretation of the words is to be admitted which suits the principle being treated.[51] Thus we have the axioms from which these considerations are derived, "*Scire leges non hoc est verba tenere, sed vim ac potestatem*";[52] "*Incivile est nisi tota lege perspecta una aliqua particula eius proposita iudicare vel respondere*";[53] "*. . . rogo non verbum ex verbo, sed sensum ex sensu transferri: quia plerumque dum proprietas verborum attenditur, sensus veritatis amittitur.*"[54]

It is necessary to pay close attention to the particles *et, vel, aut,* in order to determine whether they are to be considered disjunctively, alternatively or conjunctively.[55] Their correct use may often be discovered from the context. Thus for example, in canon 5, "*Consuetudines quae centenariae sint* ET *immemorabiles,*" must be understood as "VEL *immemorabiles.*"[56] In canon 1391, the particle *et* in the words "*sub vigilantia episcoporum et cum adnotationibus*" is to be considered conjunctively.[57]

Punctuation is sometimes of great importance. Canon 859, § 3, states, "Suadendum fidelibus ut huic praecepto (communionis paschalis) satisfaciant in sua quisque paroecia; et qui in aliena paroecia satisfecerint, curent proprium parochum de adimpleto praecepto certiorem facere." The presence of the semicolon seems to indicate that the verb *curent* does not depend on the word *suadendum,* but is in the subjunctive instead of the imperative mode.[58] Canon 120, § 2, and canon 2341 use the same

[51] Michiels, *ibid.,* p. 523.

[52] D. (1. 3) 17.

[53] D. (1. 3) 24.

[54] C. 8, X, *de verborum significatione,* V, 40.

[55] Vermeersch-Creusen, *Epitome Iuris Canonici,* I, 123; Van Hove, *De Legibus Ecclesiasticis,* p. 262.

[56] Van Hove, *ibid.,* p. 263.

[57] Pont. Intr. Comm., 20 maii 1923, ad VIII—*AAS,* XVI (1924), 115; cf. Van Hove, *ibid.,* p. 262.

[58] Vermeersch-Creusen, *op. cit.,* II, n. 128.

words, but the punctuation renders the meaning of the phrase divergent in the two cases. In canon 120, § 2 ("*Officiales maiores Romanae Curiae, ob negotia ad eorum munus pertinentia*"), the comma before the word *ob* indicates that this law applies also to the other prelates there mentioned, whereas in canon 2341, the absence of the comma before the word *ob* indicates that only the "*Officiales maiores Romanae Curiae*" are meant, and not cardinals or legates of the Holy See.[59]

Context not only refers to the proximate words of the canon but may also have reference to other canons, to other books of the code, to parts, title headings and chapter headings.[60] These are authentic parts of the Code, which indeed indicate the subject matter, but do not contain any prescriptions or prohibitions. They also may be used as a means of interpreting what is found in the subject matter.[61] There the old maxim, "*A rubro ad nigrum valet illatio*" (the inference from the rubric or title, which in the old law was in red letters, to its body, which was the ordinary black) prevails. Nevertheless the red may be derogated by the black, so that the signification of the rubrics is sometimes determined by the black; more often however the black is determined by the red.[62]

This is the first and fundamental rule of interpretation which the interpreter is bound to use in his investigation of the true sense of the law. That meaning which is deduced from the verbal formula as taken in its proper sense is presumed to be, and ordinarily is, the correct one, and no departure from this meaning is allowed unless it is manifest from elements extrinsic to the law itself that the legislator intended otherwise.[63] The writer now proposes to examine these extrinsic and secondary means in order to discover their value and utility in the interpretation of law.

59 Vermeersch-Creusen, *op. cit.*, I, n. 242, 3; Van Hove, *loc. cit.*

60 Albertus Blat, *Commentarium Textus Codicis Iuris Canonici* (6 vols., Vol. I, Romae: Ex Typographia Pontificia in Instituto Pii IX, 1921), n. 75.

61 Van Hove, *ibid.*, p. 264.

62 Van Hove, *loc. cit.*

63 Michiels, *Normae Generales Iuris Canonici*, I, 524.

CHAPTER VII

SECONDARY RULES FOR INTERPRETATION: PARALLEL TEXTS

. . . *quae si dubia et obscura manserit, ad locos Codicis parallelos, si qui sint . . . est recurrendum.*

If the proper meaning of the words remains doubtful or obscure, recourse must be had to parallel passages in the Code if there are any.

Article I. Quae si Dubia et Obscura Manserit

Ordinarily the words taken in their proper signification will reveal the intention of the legislator. Occasionally, however, the words as they sound in the legal formula may remain doubtful, or they may express the intention of the legislator in an incomplete and inadequate manner; or, even if they are clear, then because of some higher principle of reason, of justice, or of equity, they cannot be interpreted in their obvious sense. When this occurs, one must not distort the law in order to conform to the words, but one must have recourse to the secondary means of interpretation, i.e., to elements extrinsic to the verbal formula, but which are connected with it in such a manner that they prove helpful for discovering the sense of the law as intended by the legislator.[1]

Article II. Ad Locos Codicis Parallelos, si Qui Sint . . . Est Recurrendum

Among the secondary means of interpretation of any ecclesiastical law, the first one given by the Code contemplates the parallel passages or texts of the Code if such exist. Parallel texts of the Code are found in laws that have an affinity with the subject matter involved or that are expressly related to it. Here the rule holds, "*de similibus idem est iudicandum.*" It

[1] Van Hove, *De Legibus Ecclesiasticis*, p. 258.

must be noted, however, that the similarity must bear on the point at issue.[2]

All ecclesiastical laws have such manifold connections with one another that they form a juridic system. The Code is a unique organic body, and not merely a unique series of canons.[3] By bringing parallel texts together and making a comparison, one may often discover the sense of the law even though the text and context have remained doubtful. Obscure texts are to be interpreted with the aid of clearer texts, and that interpretation is to be admitted which best agrees with other laws. By the bringing together of texts, therefore, which treat of the same matter, one may from their agreement or opposition discover the sense of a doubtful text.[4]

Regarding laws enacted by the same superior, recourse to parallel passages for a better understanding of the law is readily understood, for the legislator, in making laws relating to the same discipline, even though he establishes them at different times, is presumed to act, not in an impulsive manner but reasonably, logically and coherently, always moved by the same mind and will and directed by the same general principles and concepts. This is especially true regarding the parallel laws contained in the same corpus, as in the case in the Code, especially since it was the intention of the codifier to organize the laws in a systematic manner.[5]

In practice, however, in order that the true sense of a determined law may be discovered from a comparison of the parallel passages, the process is not always the same, since the relationship between various texts may be different, as will be explained

[2] Charles Augustine, *A Commentary on the New Code of Canon Law* (8 vols., Vol. I, 4 ed., revised and enlarged, St. Louis: Herder, 1921), I, 97.

[3] John A. Abbo and Jerome D. Hannan, *The Sacred Canons* (2 vols., St. Louis: B. Herder Book Co., 1952), I, 37. For an example of this see canon 106, relating to precedence, which is to be interpreted according to the prescriptions of canons 239, § 1, 21°; 269, § 2; 280; 347; 370, § 1; 408, § 2; 478; 491; 701.

[4] Van Hove, *op. cit.*, p. 264.

[5] Michiels, *Normae Generales Iuris Canonici,* I, p. 525 Van Hove, *op. cit.*, p. 264.

in the discussions in the following sections. The contents of the various parallel passages must be understood and considered together, as bearing some relationship one to the other by reason either of harmony or of antithesis.[6]

Section 1. Argument from Agreement

First of all it may happen that full agreement results from a comparison of the texts, since they affirm or deny the same thing with substantially the same words; then without hesitation one must admit the specific sense that is established by both formulas. Again, agreement may result from a comparison of the principles, at least in so far as by different words the same principles are enumerated, or perhaps the enumerated principles supplement one another.[7] Thus from the agreement of certain texts with other dispositions of the law, that is, if a certain signification of words is in harmony with other laws on the same matter, the will of the legislator is prudently determined, since he is presumed to make laws in agreement with former laws or other laws of the same collection,[8] so that for the obscure law one must admit as true that sense (even though not strictly the proper sense) which is more in harmony with the sense of the clear law.[9] Thus by comparing canon 12 with canon 88, § 3, it becomes evident that the *usus rationis* spoken of in canon 12 means the habitual use of reason; from a comparison of canons 5 and 30, it is seen that the particle *et* in canon 5 is to be taken in a disjunctive sense, and therefore a centenary custom in canon 5 is equivalent to an immemorial custom, as is the case in canon 30.[10]

Section 2. Apparent Opposition

It may happen that from a comparison of the texts there emerges a true or at least an apparent contradiction. Since in-

[6] Michiels, *loc. cit.*

[7] Michiels, *loc. cit.*

[8] Suarez, *De Legibus*, Lib. VI, cap. I, n. 16; Michiels, *loc. cit.;* Van Hove, *op. cit.*, p. 265.

[9] Michiels, *loc. cit.*

[10] Michiels, *loc. cit.;* Van Hove, *loc. cit.*

trinsically no canon of the Code can contradict another, a solution to the apparent contradiction between them must obviously be sought. One must then examine the two laws in order to discover whether they are really opposed to each other, or whether the disagreement is merely apparent and therefore capable of solution.[11]

A: The apparent contradiction may arise from the fact that the laws belong to different periods of time.[12] In this case the principles of abrogation and derogation with reference to the former laws must be applied. In doubt the revocation of an already existing law is not presumed, but the recent laws should be adapted to the older laws and, as far as possible, made to harmonize with them.[13] Therefore, if a law understood in a determined sense can be reconciled with an earlier law, this sense, even though less proper, is to be admitted. Moreover, a more recent law, when enacted by a competent authority, abrogates a former law, if it expressly orders abrogation, or if it is directly contrary to the former law, or if it readjusts the entire subject matter of the former law, but a general law does not abolish laws enacted for particular places or the statutes of subordinate legislators unless the contrary is expressly stated in the general law, or unless the particular law was directly contrary to the new general law, as was pointed out in canon 6, 1°, in reference to laws existing before the Code.[14]

B: Again, perhaps the opposition which seemed to exist at first sight is only apparent because the laws refer to matters which are quite distinct and based on altogether different suppositions. Thus there is no opposition between canon 3, which recognizes the right of patronage conceded to different nations by concordats, and canon 1471, which declares that the right of patronage conceded in concordats must be understood as merely the right to present a certain candidate, and not as the right of

[11] Abbo-Hannan, *The Sacred Canons,* I, 37.

[12] This source of apparent contradiction would not apply to the canons originally in the Code, since they were promulgated at the same time. Cf. Abbo-Hannan, *loc. cit.*

[13] Canon 23.

[14] Canon 22; cf. Van Hove, *De Legibus Ecclesiasticis,* p. 265.

patronage in the proper sense of the word. These laws are easily reconciled. Canon 3 refers to concordats entered into in the past, while canon 1471 refers to future concordats.[15]

C: It may happen that one law is general and the other special. Then, of course, since *generi per speciem derogatur*,[16] the general law retains its force in all cases and in regard to all subjects not coming under the special law.[17] Thus, although ordinary power can be delegated (canon 199, § 1), the canon penitentiary cannot delegate to others the ordinary power of confessional jurisdiction that he has (canon 401, § 1), nor can the pastor delegate his jurisdiction for the hearing of confessions (canons 874-880).[18]

D: One law may state a principle, the other an exception. Then one must apply the principle, *exceptio firmat regulam in contrarium pro casibus non exceptis*. A particular disposition, while it excepts a certain case or cases from the law, really declares and confirms the law concerning things not excepted, for then there exists the so called *argumentum a contrario*, by which, from an exception made by the legislator, one argues to the universality or the generality of that law.[19] Thus, for example, canon 458, § 4, states that, in countries where the conferring of parishes is done by means of a concursus, that form shall be retained, but according to canon 2162 a pastor may be transferred to another parish if the transfer is judged by the ordinary to be to the advantage of the diocese. The question could arise

[15] Michiels, *op. cit.*, I, 525; Van Hove, *op. cit.*, p. 267.

[16] Reg. 34, R. J., in VI°.

[17] Canon 6, 1°, and canon 22; Van Hove, *op. cit.*, p. 265; Michiels seems to be less exact in his application of this principle: ". . . examinandum est: num forsan *una lex non sit generalis, altera vero specialis,* quod praesertim verificatur in concursu legis Superioris cum lege inferioris; tunc sane, cum 'genere per speciem derogetur,' lex generalis valorem suum retinet quoad omnes casus et subditos per legem specialem non expresse ordinatos."—*Ibid.*, p. 256. From these words one might receive the impression that, even if the law of the subordinate legislator is contrary to the law of the superior, the law of the former would ordinarily prevail.

[18] Pont. Intr. Comm., 16 oct. 1919, ad III—*AAS*, XI (1919), p. 477; Van Hove, *op. cit.*, p. 266.

[19] Michiels, *loc. cit.*

whether the pastor thus transferred had to acquire the parish *per viam concursus* according to canon 459, § 4, or could acquire it apart from a concursus. This difficulty one solves by admitting canon 2162 as an exception to canon 495, § 4, and therefore in the case of a transfer for the good of the diocese a concursus is not required.[20]

This rule in itself is clear, but it is replete with practical difficulties and dangers, and therefore is to be used with the utmost caution, for it is not always easy to determine which law constitutes a general rule and which stands as an exception. If both the principle and the exception (or exceptions) as such are stated explicitly in the law, there is no reason why one cannot use the *argumentum a contrario*. An example of explicit exception is found in canon 45. Rescripts when signalized with the phrase *motu proprio* are valid even though certain truths which otherwise should have been stated in the petition are suppressed, unless there is alleged only one motivating reason which at the same time is false, *salvo praescripto can. 1054*. Canon 1054 states that a dispensation from a matrimonial impediment of minor degree is not invalidated either through the statement of a falsehood or through the concealment of the truth, even though the only one motivating reason advanced is false.[21]

An exception is implicit if in some other way it can be proved that some specific disposition of law has the character of a general rule, so that the latter suffers derogation from this disposition of law in a particular matter.[22]

From whether or not this principle, scil., the exception evinces the rule, can be verified in a case under consideration depends the solution of the question, *an inclusio unius sit exclusio alterius*, that is, whether a law when treating of some matter does or does not treat of another matter in the same way. For example, canon 1099 exempts heretics from the law regarding the canonical form for the contracting of matrimony. Is it valid to conclude that they are therefore bound to obey the other ecclesi-

[20] S.C.C., *Romana et Aliarum*, 21 iun. 1919—*AAS*, XI (1919), 318-321; Van Hove, *loc. cit.*; Michiels, *loc. cit.*

[21] Michiels, *ibid.*, pp. 526-527; Van Hove, *loc. cit.*

[22] Van Hove, *loc. cit.*

astical laws which pertain to matrimony? Canon 12 states that non-baptized persons are not bound by purely ecclesiastical laws. Is it correct to deduce from this that all baptized persons over seven years of age and having the use of reason are bound by ecclesiastical laws? It must not be forgotten that the rule (the exception evinces the rule) can be validly applied only when it is apparent from the context or from parallel texts that a certain law deflects from the general rules or principles of law, or when it is certain that the law is to be understood in a restrictive sense, in other words, as often as the inclusion of one implies the exclusion of the other.[23] Thus in canon 1099, § 2, from the fact that heretics are by the law expressly exempted from the observance of the canonical form for the contracting of matrimony, *a contrario* it is licit to conclude that they are bound by the other marriage laws of the Church, since from canon 12 and 87 the general principle is clear, so that canon 1099, § 2, stands as an exception.[24]

On the other hand, the same argument from canon 12 in regard to the non-baptized would not be correct, because inherently (*per se*) the general exclusion of all the non-baptized does not mean the inclusion of all the baptized, since this is nowhere stated in the positive law.[25] Again, it would be wrong to argue to the existence of a general law invalidating every rescript asked for in bad faith from the fact that the concealing in bad faith of some irregularity or censure nullifies the validity of a rescript which concedes a general dispensation from irregularities or a general absolution from censures. The reason is that here the question deals not with a case of a general rule and an exception to the rule, but simply with a case wherein the law ordains differently on different things. When however the law rules on something *modo taxativo,* the principle, *inclusio unius*

[23] ". . . quoties inclusio unius, id est rei quam in casu lex permittit aut vetat aut iubet, est quasi exceptio iuris alias preacipientis vel vetantis vel permittentis."—D'Annibale, *Summula Theologiae Moralis,* Pars I, *Prolegomena* (5. ed., Romae, 1908), n. 185, nota 25; Van Hove, *loc. cit.*

[24] Michiels, *ibid.*, p. 528.

[25] Michiels, *loc. cit.*

est exclusio alterius, is valid; but when the law speaks *modo exemplativo,* this principle does not apply. Canons 1043, 1044, 1045 are to be understood *modo taxativo,* that is, the power of dispensation extends *only* to the cases mentioned in these canons. Canon 33, § 1, allows one to follow different times in the fulfillment of four different private obligations. In this case *inclusio unius est exclusio alterius* may not be used, because it is not certain whether the cases are enumerated *modo taxativo* or *exemplativo.*[26]

Section 3. Improper Sense

If the parallel texts understood in their proper signification are truly contrary and one cannot overcome the opposition in the ways indicated above, the proper signification of the words must be abandoned for a less proper sense which will forestall contradiction, as long as this improper sense is not positively unreasonable, opposed to certain affirmations of the legislator, or contrary to principles adhered to by him. In this manner the legislator is shown to be more reasonable than he would be if he enacted two opposing laws which cannot possibly be observed at the same time. In this case it is, therefore, to be presumed that he does not intend that which is expressed by the proper signification, but rather that which sound logic, harmony of laws, and proper administration demand.[27] *"Verba ita sunt intelligenda ut res de qua agitur valere possit potius quam perire."* [28]

Section 4. True Opposition

True opposition is conceivable between the laws of a superior and a subordinate legislator. In this hypothesis, the laws of the superior must prevail, unless the superior legislator provides for an exception, whence there would be no opposition.

If the same superior enacts two laws which are mutually exclusive, intending that both be simultaneously in force, it must be said that they are in true opposition and are therefore desti-

[26] Michiels, *ibid.,* p. 527; Van Hove, *ibid.,* p. 267.

[27] Van Hove, *loc. cit.;* Michiels, *loc. cit.*

[28] C. 25, X, *de verborum significatione,* V, 40.

tute of all binding force.[29] This possibility, however, is difficult to imagine.

Section 5. The General Principles of Law

The general principles of law may be considered as similar to the principles regarding parallel passages. What has been said regarding the logical coherence of parallel laws is true also, but perhaps in a lesser degree, of the principles of law and the rules of law.

One may distinguish between the principles of law and the rules of law. A principle of law is a moral source from which positive legislation arises. The juridical order is part of the moral order, so that all positive legislation must reflect the principles of the moral law.[30] Occasionally, therefore, these principles may serve as an aid in interpretation, since the legislator's enactments are expected to correspond to and be guided by these higher principles of morality and right reason. These principles, however, since they, for the most part, are abstract and do not directly enter into the will of the legislator, are to be cautiously used by the interpreter.[31]

The rules of law on the other hand are constructed by the law itself. There are two different ways in which a rule of law can be constructed. The first is through the extracting of a common element as found in several laws: [32] the second is through the establishment of a presumption as based upon past facts.[33] The

[29] Van Hove, *loc. cit.;* Abbo-Hannan, *The Sacred Canons,* I, 37.

[30] Edward Roelker, "An Introduction to the Rules of Law," *The Jurist,* X (1950), 273 (hereafter cited as Roelker).

[31] Michiels, *ibid.,* p. 529.

[32] "Reiffenstuel cites examples where the stigma of infamy bars one from a prelacy, a benefice, the duties of a judge or a magistrate, etc. These laws are found in different places in the Decretals, but in every case the penalty of infamy is a disqualification. Hence, to indicate this status of disqualification in every pertinent law a Rule was constructed which briefly stated that infamy is a disqualification. The Rule reads: *Infamibus portae non pateant dignitatum.*"—Roelker, p. 276, citing Reiffenstuel, *Ius Canonicum* (5 vols. in 7, Parisiis, 1864-1870), Vol. VII, p. 2, n. 8, and Reg. 87, R. J., in VI°.

[33] "Reiffenstuel says that perjurers are not admitted to testify because of

rules thus established become applicable to many laws. Many of these were incorporated into the Old Canon Law and some into the New.[34] Since they are in accord with the whole juridical system of the Church, it is easy to understand how they may be used and applied as parallels. Those rules of law which are found in the Code are authentic and are to be evaluated according to the interpretation of the approved authors of the old law.[35] The others, though not authentic, have considerable doctrinal value.

One must beware of using as objective principles the axioms taken from jurists and interpreters, since these are often bound up with their own personal philosophical and juridical concepts. In many cases they are purely subjective, and in no way enter into the mind of the legislator. Therefore, as a means of interpretation they are to be rejected.[36]

SCHOLION

It is appropriate here to note that canon 18, since it refers to the interpretation of all ecclesiastical laws and not merely to those of the Code, intends that the parallel laws of the Code be used also as a means of interpretation for laws made by subordinate legislators. The subordinate legislator is presumed to act in accordance with established law and the general juridic system.[37] This juridic principle is definitely expressed in the words of canon 18. *"Leges ecclesiasticae"* (therefore also the ecclesiastical laws of a subordinate legislator), if their meaning remains doubtful after the application of the proper signification

---

suspicion of further perjury. Again he says that a woman who has left her husband because of his cruelty need not return to him because of the fear of further cruelty. In both cases a presumption of repeated immoral acts exists. This presumption is contained in the Rule: *Semel malus semper praesumitur esse malus."*—Roelker, pp. 277-278, citing Reiffenstuel, *op. cit.*, Vol. VII, p. 1, n. 4, and Reg. 8, R. J., in VI°

[34] See especially the footnotes of the *Normae Generales,* the first book of the Code.

[35] Canon 6, n. 2.

[36] Michiels, *Normae Generales Iuris Canonici,* I, 530.

[37] Cicognani, *Canon Law,* p. 611.

to the words, are to be examined in the light of the laws of the Code which refer to the same or similar matters.

Therefore, in a case of doubt or obscurity, the words of any given particular law must be explained in such a manner that there will eventuate not any discrepancy between the universal law and the particular law, but rather harmony and agreement.[38] This principle has always obtained in ecclesiastical law. It has the effect of making the universal law a part, so to speak, of the particular law in a given instance.[39]

[38] Ernricus Pirhing, *Ius Canonicum in V Libros Decretalium* (4 vols., Dilingae, 1722), Lib. I, tit. 2, n. CV: "Ubi aliquid a iure communi discrepari videtur, reducendum est ad ius commune si fieri potest, ne pereat, quia promptum est leges legibus concordare."—*Glossa s. v. Iuri communi,* ad c. 8, X, *de consuetudine,* I, 4.

[39] . . . quia quod dicitur statutum habet et recipit interpretationem passivam a iure communi, operatur per relationem ad ius commune perinde ac si ius commune esset insertum et incorporatum in statuto."—Tuschus, *Practicae Conclusiones,* VI, Litt. R, Concl. 129. Cf. Schmidt, *The Principles of Authentic Interpretation in Canon 17 of the Code of Canon Law,* pp. 142-144.

CHAPTER VIII

THE PURPOSE AND CIRCUMSTANCES OF THE LAW AND THE MIND OF THE LEGISLATOR

. . . *quae si dubia et obscura manserit . . . ad legis finem ac circumstantias et ad mentem legislatoris est recurrendum.*

If the proper meaning of the words remains doubtful and obscure, recourse must be had to the purpose and circumstances of the law, and to the mind of the legislator.

Article I. The Purpose of the Law

The purpose of the law or the *ratio legis* is the purpose for which the legislator enacts the law. However it is necessary to distinguish a twofold reason for law. One is called the intrinsic reason, or the *causa finalis,* or the *finis operis.* The other is extrinsic to the law, and is called the motivating cause, or the *finis operantis.*[1] The *finis operis* of the law is that specific good to which the law tends of its very nature. This is intrinsic to the law and is always the same. Every law must be interpreted according to the *finis operis,* since otherwise it would be useless or superfluous.

However, the legislator in making a law may have other reasons besides the *finis operis,* reasons extrinsic to the law itself, but considered by the legislator as necessary or useful to the common good. These extrinsic reasons are called the *finis operantis.*[2] If this end (the *finis operantis*) can be discovered, it may be of considerable assistance to the interpreter in ascertaining the true sense of a law when its meaning is obscure.[3]

The proper use of this means of interpretation, however, as also

[1] Van Hove, *De Legibus Ecclesiasticis,* p. 268; Michiels, *Normae Generales Iuris Canonici,* I, 533.

[2] For example, the *finis operis* of the law of fasting is the acquisition of the virtue of temperance; the *finis operantis* could be penance or mortification.—Suarez, *De Legibus,* Lib. VI, cap. V, n. 7.

[3] Van Hove, *op. cit.,* p. 268.

its application to individual cases, involves a great many difficulties so that the interpreter is warned to proceed with extreme caution lest he fall into serious error. Doubtlessly the juridical end intended by the legislator can at times be known with certainty, either inasmuch as he has expressed it in the law itself, or inasmuch as it has been manifested in the acts preparatory to the drafting of the law, or inasmuch as the reason was given in the old law from which the new law was taken.[4] Suarez maintained that, when the reason for the law is expressed in the law itself, there is a very good indication of the mind of the legislator, which indication would hold second place among the means of interpretation, since in this case the reason for the law is, so to speak, part of it.[5] Nevertheless, even though the reason for the law be expressed in the law, it is not an infallible indication of the mind of the legislator, unless all other circumstances are weighed, since even the reason manifested in the law may not be clearly expressed. Again it may happen that the same reason moved the mind in different ways toward different objects, and therefore to fully know the mind of the legislator one may be without a sufficient means even though the reason for the law has been expressed by the legislator, so that some other means of interpretation needs to be invoked.[6] Finally, it may happen that the reason given for the enactment of the law is not the only one that the legislator had in mind. He may have had other reasons, which he has not manifested in the law.[7]

When the reason for the law is not manifested, jurists naturally speculate as to what might have motivated the legislator and caused him to enact the law. Though this method often con-

[4] However, if the new law differs somewhat from the old, it may well be that some new reason has prompted the legislator to make the change. In this case the reasons found in the old law would lose some of their force as a means of interpretation.

[5] "At vero quando ratio legis in ipsa lege continetur, magnum indicium esse potest mentis legislatoris, et post verba ipsa videtur secundum certitudinis locum obtinere, quia tunc ratio legis est aliquo modo pars eius."—*De Legibus,* Lib. VI, cap. I, n. 20.

[6] Suarez, *De Legibus,* Lib. VI, cap. I, n. 20.

[7] Michiels, *op. cit.,* I, 540.

tributes some help, it must be classified as mere conjecture, and not as a certain indication of the reason for the law, for the reason thus alleged exists with certainty only in the mind of the commentator, and though it may *de facto* be a reason for the law, it is still quite possible that it is not the only reason, or the reason that actually moved the legislator to make the law.[8]

Suarez and Michiels proceeded to solve this problem in two different ways. Both however achieved the same results.[9]

Suarez employed what might be called the inductive method. He examined the doubtful case (which may or may not fall under the scope of the law) and, by comparing it with other cases which certainly were comprehended in the law, decided whether or not the inclusion of the doubtful case was necessary in order that the purpose of the law might be fulfilled. If he found an identity of reason (together with certain other conditions to be explained in the following pages) for both the certain and the doubtful cases, he concluded that the doubtful case fell under the scope of the law. In this case the axiom obtained: *"Ubi eadem est ratio legis, ibi eadem est legis dispositio."* On the other hand, if after having examined the doubtful case he discovered that only a similarity of reason existed between it and the certain cases, he concluded that the doubtful case was not included in the law.[10]

Michiels, on the other hand, solved the problem through the use of the deductive method, declaring that first of all the end of the law is to be directly examined. When one has discovered what the end or reason of the law positively demands, one deduces *per modum consequentiae* that the legislator intended to include or exclude the case which is under consideration. This method of interpretation does not extend the will of the legislator to the particular case, but it extends only the sense of the words so that the case will be included.[11]

[8] Suarez, *De Legibus,* Lib. VI, cap. I, n. 20; Van Hove, *op. cit.,* p. 269. It is to be noted that the reason for the law is very seldom found stated in the Code.

[9] Suarez, *De Legibus,* Lib. VI, cap. III, nn. 1-22; Michiels, *op. cit.,* I, 541-552.

[10] Suarez, *De Legibus,* Lib. VI, cap. III, nn. 9-23.

[11] Michiels, *ibid.,* pp. 543-544.

The problem to be solved is this: When and to what extent is recourse to the *finis legis* permitted or even necessary, in order that the true sense of a certain law be determined, that is, in order that there be determined what objects and what subjects are included under the words of the law, and therefore subject to it according to the mind of the legislator *vi propria*? In other words, it is a case of true interpretation of an existing law, and not of supplying for the silence of the legislator. (See canon 20.)

Two hypotheses are to be considered.

1) A law is interpreted according to the proper sense of the words. The reason for the law is called upon for the disclosure of whether the sense indicated by the proper signification of the words (and therefore presumably true) is confirmed or denied. It is discovered that the *ratio legis* confirms the sense indicated by the words. In such a procedure, then, no difficulty is encountered.

2) A law is interpreted according to the proper sense of the words, but the *ratio legis* indicates that this sense is not the one intended by the legislator. Herein lies the difficulty. When does the *ratio legis* prevail over the proper *sensus verborum* and vice versa?

Section 1. Extension of Law

First of all, a law may exist whose end or reason is known, but whose application to a particular case, if interpreted according to the proper signification of the words, would fail to achieve this end. Is it true that the will of the legislator as expressed in a certain law extends to all cases for which the same reason exists, even the cases not comprehended within the proper signification of the words of the law? In other words, is the principle, *"Ubi eadem est ratio legis, ibi eadem est legis dispositio,"* valid?

A. General Principle

The law, fundamentally (*per se*), is not to be extended because of a similarity or identity of reason,[12] since the legislator may

[12] "Nam in iis quae pendent a libra voluntate legislatoris, non concluditur *a pari aut a maiori ad minus*. Ratio enim legis non est ipsa lex et silentium legislatoris facile importat exclusionem illorum quae sub silentio

enact a law regarding one matter and not intend to include other matters, even though a similar reason be found for both cases. For it may happen that it is not necessary for the legislator to dispose of all similar things in the same manner, and he may choose one matter rather than another.[13] The will of the legislator is always of its very nature indicated by the verbal formula as taken in the proper signification of the words, and therefore only those things can be said to be willed by the legislator which are expressed in the words of the law.[14] Therefore that method is to be rejected as abusive and contrary to the nature of law which neglects the verbal formula or considers it as something secondary, and attempts to determine the meaning of the law from the purpose of the law alone.[15]

B. Exception

The law, beyond the cases certainly included under the proper signification of the words, includes also *all* those cases but *only* those which, though not comprehended under the proper signification of the words, are, however, *objectively necessary for the adequate fulfillment of the end which was beyond doubt intended by the legislator when he made the law.*[16]

Special consideration is to be given to the following:

1) The inclusion of the case in question must be *objectively necessary* for the fulfillment of the end, i.e., not merely useful or helpful to the easier attainment of the end, but such that, if it

---

premuntur, nec absque ratione cogente est recedendum a proprio sensu verborum."—Van Hove, *De Legibus Ecclesiasticis,* p. 270.

13 "Et ideo necessarium non est, nec moraliter verum aut ordinarium, quod voluntas legislatoris extendatur ad omnia in quibus potest inveniri similis ratio. Quia voluntas pro sua libertate potest circa unam materiam disponere, et non circa aliam, licet in utraque inveniatur similis ratio, quia fortasse non expedit in omnibus disponere, et pro suo arbitrio legislator eligit unam materiam potius quam aliam."—Suarez, *De Legibus,* Lib. VI, cap. III, n. 12.

14 "Quod voluit expressit, quod noluit tacuit . . ."—D. (1, 20) 14; Michiels, *ibid.,* p. 541.

15 Michiels, *loc. cit.*

16 Michiels, *loc. cit.*

were not included, the principal end desired by the legislator would actually be impeded and the law would be rendered useless or even unreasonable and unjust.[17]

2) *The end intended by the legislator,* that is, the end which was in itself and by itself sufficient to effectively move the legislator to make the law, even though the inclusion of the case in question would not have been necessary for the attainment of the secondary ends which may also have been intended by the legislator. On the other hand, if the inclusion of the case in question had been necessary for the attainment of the secondary end, but not the primary end of the law, it was to be considered as outside the scope of the law.[18]

3) *The end beyond doubt intended by the legislator,* for it must be certain that the end was actually and principally intended by the legislator. This may be konwn either because the reason for the law has been stated in the law itself, or because there exists some other means, such as an authentic interpretation. Thus reasons or ends speculatively contemplated by private interpreters would not fulfill this condition. However, Suarez stated that the reason need not always be expressed in the law before it can be certainly known.[19]

4) The *adequate fulfillment* of the end intended by the legislator, that is, all those cases must be included which are necessary if the complete and total end which motivated the legislator is to be achieved. Therefore, if the end intended by the legislator

[17] Michiels, *loc. cit.*

[18] Suarez, *De Legibus,* Lib. VI, cap. III, n. 19-20.

[19] ". . . potest sufficienter constare de ratione legis, etiam si scripta non sit; ergo idem operabitur . . . (ac·ratio scripta) . . . quia non habet dictum effectum quia scripta est, sed quia in se talia est. Nihilominus tamen quia quando est scripta, pars est legis, et de illa certissime constat, et per contextum constare etiam potest, quomodo determinet alia verba legis, ideo regulariter vix habet locum cum obligatione haec extensio ex vi rationis, nisi scripta sit. Quando vero non est scripta, juxta legis qualitatem et materiam poterit extensio fieri cum maiore vel minore certitudine praesumptionis, et interdum poterit esse tam evidens, vel communiter recepta, ut ad obligationem legis sufficiat."—Suarez, *De Legibus,* Lib. VI, cap. IV, n. 6. Cf. also Tuschus, *Practicae Conclusiones,* VI, Litt. R, concl. 30, n. 5; Panormitanus, *Commentaria,* Lib. I, tit. III (*de rescriptis*), cap. *Quia nonulli,* n. 10; Michiels, *ibid.,* p. 542.

can be adequately fulfilled apart from the inclusion of these cases, they are not to be included; if, however, by the exclusion of these doubtful cases the end could be only partially fulfilled, they are to be included.[20]

The reason why the cases described above are contained in the law is this: every law is presumed to be just, and enacted by the legislator in a prudent and suitable manner, but it would not be such unless it would be capable of adequately attaining the end for which it was established,[21] that is, unless it included, over and above the cases expressed by the words, all other cases (even though not expressed) which are equally necessary for the attainment of the primary end of the law. According to Michiels, when the *ratio legis* or the motivating end of the law demands it, the law is to be extended not only to cases included in the widest and most improper sense of the words, but even to cases which are in no way comprehended by the words.[22] The given explanation stresses the fact that it is more reasonable to presume that the legislator was imprudent in his choice of words, than to admit that his law is absurd, unjust or useless. Therefore in this sense is to be understood the rule of law, *"certum est, quod is committit in legem, qui, legis verba complectens, contra legis nitur voluntatem."* [23]

On the other hand, *only* those cases are included which are truly necessary for the adequate attainment of the end of the law,

[20] Michiels, *loc. cit.*

[21] Suarez, *De Legibus,* Lib. VI, cap. III, n. 22.

[22] "Nec restringatur hoc principium ad soles casus inter *aliquem* saltem verborum sensum, utut remotiorem, imo omnino latum et forsan improprium, contentos, . . . ; licet enim legislatoris voluntas, quae sola intrinsice determinat legis vim obligatoriam, regulariter et directe manifestetur per verba ab ipso adhibita, non tamen semper per verba sola, sed aliquando et per finem legis indubitanter panditur; iamvero, quando *voluntas* illa ex fine manifestata ad injustitiam vel absurditatem vel circumventionem legis vitandam requirit, ut extendatur ad alios quoque casus, sub verbis, etiam latissime intellectis, nullatenus comprehensos, tunc voluntati ejus restrictae, per verba inadaequate circumscriptae, indubitanter praevalere debet voluntas ejus magis extensa et adaequata, per considerationem finis imposita."—Michiels, *op. cit.,* I, 542-543.

[23] Reg. 88, R. J., in VI°.

because, even though the same reason may exist for two different cases, the legislator may choose one and not the other, if the one in itself proves sufficient for attaining the primary end intended by the legislator.[24]

This method, employed by Michiels, seems to be more in conformity with the true concept of interpretation in the proper sense of the word, for if the *finis legis* (that end which of itself was the principal motivating cause of the law, apart from other secondary ends) is certainly known, a comparatively simple reasoning process will show what cases are essential for the attainment of that end, and therefore included in the will of the legislator. Thus, though the signification of the words is extended to include a case which the very purpose of the law calls for, the intention of the legislator is in no way extended, since the end itself indicates this extent.[25]

Suarez, on the other hand, by examining the case in question and comparing it with other cases which certainly fall under the scope of the law, seemed to be interpreting by analogy, which method could possibly suppose that the intention of the legislator did not *de facto* extend to the doubtful case, but presumably would do so by analogy according to principles which are now accepted in canon 20 of the Code.

C. Practical Application

The foregoing principle is verified generally:

1) In *correlatives,* in so far as they are truly correlatives, that is, as having a mutual or reciprocal relation, in such a sense

[24] ". . . quia lex pendet a voluntate, voluntas autem pro sua libertate potest unum velle et non aliud, etiamsi in utro sit eadem ratio volendi."—Suarez, *De Legibus,* Lib. VI, cap. III, n. 20.

[25] Canon 18 does not seem to demand that the proper signification of the words be *always* strictly observed. "Tam ex jurisprudentia quam ex doctrina admodum certum est non deesse leges, de quibus invicte constat earum verba a legislatore non adhibita fuisse sensu proprio admodum inaequivoco, sed sensu ab ea plus minusve diverso, ultra sensum proprium scilicet extenso vel, e contra, infra illum restricto, vel imo sensu aliquatenus improprio. (Sufficiat conferre varias interpretationes authenticas a competente auctoritate datas!)"—Michiels, *Normae Generales Iuris Canonici,* I, 474.

namely that the existence of one necessarily implies the existence of the other. For example, husband and wife are correlative terms, and when the law grants a partial divorce, that is, separation from bed and board because of the wife's adultery, the wife is granted the same if her husband is guilty of adultery. The alienator and the buyer of ecclesiastical goods are correlatives, so that if one is forbidden to sell the other is forbidden to buy (canon 1530).[26]

2) In matters that are so *connected* that one cannot exist without the other. Thus, if a person is permitted, for a just reason, to request the sacraments from a priest who is excommunicated, he is permitted by the same law to administer them (canon 2261, § 2). He who may conduct a trial can compel the parties to appear in court. Thus canon 66, § 3, decrees that faculties granted to anyone include also such powers as are necessary for their exercise.[27] Negatively: *"Cum quid prohibetur, prohibentur omnia, quae sequuntur ex illo."*[28] Thus, he who is not allowed to contract matrimony is not allowed to enter a betrothal.[29]

3) In matters which are *equivalent* by law, even though no similarity exists. Thus it is seen from canon 1251, § 1, that in matters of fast and abstinence, eggs and milk products are considered equivalent; in some respects, at least, minors and moral persons are considered equivalent (canon 100, § 3); and election to and postulation for office are considered equivalent (canon 179). It seems to be true, however, that in cases wherein the legislator expressly declares that two things are equivalent, v.g., in canon 451, § 2, the law does not merely *extend* to the equivalent object but actually comprehends it under the *proper signification* of the words. Thus it seems that even in *odiosis* the equivalent object is to be included.[30]

[26] Cicognani, *Canon Law*, p. 611; Michiels, *op. cit.*, I, 545; Maroto, *Institutiones Iuris Canonici*, I, 254; Van Hove, *De Legibus Ecclesiasticis*, p. 271.

[27] Cicognani, *op. cit.*, p. 612; Michiels, *loc. cit.;* Maroto, *loc. cit.;* Van Hove, *loc. cit.*

[28] Reg. 39, R. J., in VI°.

[29] Michiels, *ibid.*, pp. 545, 546; Maroto, *loc. cit.;* Cicognani, *loc. cit.*

[30] Michiels, *ibid.*, p. 547.

4) In things *contained* within the object of the law, that is, when the law pertains to a certain object, it also pertains to all matters which are contained within that object, as a conclusion is contained within a principle, a species in a genus, a part in the whole, or that which is less in that which is greater. For example, one who is capable of making a will, is also capable of making a bequest, or one who can dispense from vows, can also commute them. However as Michiels and D'Annibale (1815-1892) pointed out, matters pertaining to this category are also comprehended under the proper signification of the words, so that if the object of the law is known, everything contained within that object is also known.[31]

5) In matters *exemplified* in law, that is, in instances wherein the law does not intend to enumerate all possible cases, but gives several of the more frequent cases as examples. Thus canon 2147 gives a number of reasons why an irremovable pastor may nevertheless be removed from the pastoral office. By this the legislator does not mean to exclude other reasons which may also suffice for his removal.[32]

There is no doubt that the foregoing principle (when all conditions are verified beyond doubt) can be applied in these cases *in favorabilibus*. However, canon 19 states that laws which decree a penalty, or restrict the free exercise of one's rights, or establish an exception to the law, are subject to a strict interpretation, and canon 2219, § 3, warns that a penalty may not be extended from person to person, or from one case to another, though there is the same or even a greater reason for holding the person guilty. May the *finis legis* ever call upon a law to allow for its extension beyond the proper sense of the words *in odiosis?*

Authors disagree to some extent on this matter. Suarez held that in some cases the *finis legis* could demand that the law receive an extensive interpretation even in penal matters. He explained that a comprehensive interpretation could be twofold, one of necessity, the other of congruity. When it was a case of

[31] Michiels, *ibid.*, p. 546; D'Annibale, *Summula Theologiae Moralis*, Pars I, *Prolegomena*, n. 186, nota 36.

[32] Van Hove, *op. cit.*, p. 279; Michiels, *ibid.*, p. 547.

necessity, that is, when it was necessary to preserve the efficacy and justice of the law, then penal as well as favorable laws were to allow for extension. When it was a case of congruity, that is, when the justice and prudence of the law could be maintained without allowance for the extension, then the penal laws could not be extended.[33]

Reiffenstuel proceeded a step further. He taught that a penal law must be extended in consequence of any adequate reason if it was expressed in the law, in consequence at least of the fact that solely one certified reason called for the existence of the law. He seemed to abstract completely from the accompanying element of necessity in the case.[34]

D'Annibale contended that the law was to be extended even *in odiosis,* if otherwise an evident intolerable absurdity would follow.[35]

Van Hove approved the opinion of Suarez. "Verior est doctrina F. Suarezii, qui latam admittit interpretationem, quam vocat extensivam comprehensivam, quae remanet intra sensum aliqualem verborem non tamen magis coarctatum, quando haec

[33] "Dico ergo extensionem comprehensivam duplicem distingui, unam necessitatis, aliam congruitatis . . . , unam omnino necessariam ad justitiam vel rectitudinem et in gratiam observantium legis, aliam non necessariam seu voluntariam, quia licet in uno sensu possit lex multa comprehendere juste et sine inconvenientia, alia minor comprehensio sufficit ad justitiam legis et proprietatem verborum cum ratione etiam legis servandam. Dico ergo generales illas regulas de non ampliandis legibus poenalibus (aliisque odiosis et correctoriis) intelligi de interpretatione, ut ita dicam, voluntaria, id est, sine qua potest conservari prudens dispositio et justitia legis, quia infra hanc latitudinem benigne semper est interpretanda lex poenalis. Quando vero extensio est necessaria ad justitiam legis, secus est; ideoque merito dicunt multi ex dictis auctoribus, hanc comprehensionem non esse propriam extensionem, sed adaequatam legis interpretationem, quae in poenalibus etaim servanda est."—Suarez, *De Legibus,* Lib. VI, cap. IV, n. 3. Again he stated: "Praeterea debet intelligi quando talis comprehensio ex vi rationis necessaria est ut vere et integre impleatur ratio legis, vel ut sit justa et rationabilis, ut explicatum est, tunc enim est evidens necessitas, quia non minus efficax et justa ac rationabilis debet esse plenalis quam quaelibet alia."—*Op. cit.,* Lib. VI, cap. IV, n. 2.

[34] *Ius Canonicum Universum,* Lib. I, tit. II, nn. 427-434.

[35] *Summula Theologiae Moralis,* Pars I, *Prolegomena,* n. 309.

comprehensio non congruens quidem sed necessaria est ut vere et integre impleatur ratio legis, ne lex fiat inutilis vel illusoria." [36] D'Annibale,[37] Cicognani,[38] Maroto (1875-1937),[39] and others have called for the extension of those laws which have always received an extensive interpretation from the approved authors.

On the other hand, others have rejected any extension of penal laws in consequence of any identity of reason.[40] Alphonsus de Castro (1495-1558)[41] taught that the punishment attaching to penal laws depended altogether on the free will of the legislator, and therefore could not be extended from one case to another in view of any identity of reason.

This problem is ably solved by Michiels through the use of the same principle which has been stated above: odious laws, beyond those cases which are certainly included in the proper signification of the words, include also all but at the same time only such cases which are so necessary for the adequate attainment of the end, if beyond doubt it was intended by the legislator, that unless they be considered as truly comprehended in the law *vi propria*, the law itself would become useless or illusory or unreasonable or unjust.[42] The reason is this: the interpretation of any law, whether favorable or odious, must be reasonable and just; but it would not be such if there were excluded from the law such cases which, even though not included under the proper signification of the words of the law, are absolutely necessary for the attainment of the primary and motivating end of the law, and therefore were most certainly intended by the legislator.[43]

[36] Van Hove, *De Legibus Ecclesiasticis,* p. 310.

[37] *Summula Theologiae Moralis,* Pars I, *Prolegomena,* n. 309.

[38] *Canon Law,* p. 612.

[39] *Institutiones Iuris Canonici,* I, 254.

[40] Roncaglia, *Moralis Theologia Universa* (3 vols., Venetiis, 1760), Tr. III, q. 4, cap. 2; Salmanticenses, *Cursus Theologiae Moralis,* (6 vols. in 4, Venetiis, 1714-1728), III, tr. IV, n. 39; Michael Lega, *Praelectiones in Textum Iuris Canonici, De Iudiciis Ecclesiasticis* (4 vols., Romae, 1896-1901), Lib. II, Vol. III (1899), n. 79.

[41] *De potestate legis poenalis* (Parisiis, 1587), Lib. I, cap. 7, fo. 39.

[42] Michiels, *Normae Generales Iuris Canonici,* I, 552.

[43] Suarez, *De Legibus,* Lib. VI, cap. IV, n. 3; Michiels, *loc. cit.*

Strict interpretation is not the product of a consideration of the words of the law alone. Strict interpretation, like any other type of interpretation, must be determined not only from the words of the law, but also, when these are doubtful, from the end of the law and the mind of the legislator. Canon 19 decrees that penalties, restrictions of rights, and exceptions to the law, are to receive a strict interpretation. But is not that a strict interpretation which demands that only those cases be included that are absolutely necessary for the preservation of the law against frustration and injustice? When this principle is stated in a positive manner, it may seem at first glance to be somewhat severe. However, it is substantially the same teaching that was offered by the eminent canonists of the old and the new law. Its conclusions are reached by means of a true interpretation, and not by analogy or comparison. Canon 2219, § 3, prohibits the extension of penalties from person to person or from one case to another, but this prohibition presupposes a *comparison* of cases; on the other hand, in the use of this principle, the case in question is examined in reference to the *end* of the law, and if this canont be attained apart from the inclusion of the case in question, then indeed it must be included. *'Certum est, quod is committat in legem, qui legis verba complectens, contra legis nititur voluntatem."* [44]

Section 2. Restriction of Law

What is to be done in a situation wherein the meaning of the words, if taken in their proper signification, would comprehend more than the known end intended by the legislator?

The presumption is that the words employed by the legislator, when interpreted according to the norms of canons 18 and 19, will clearly indicate the cases which he considers necessary or useful for the attainment of his purpose. However, let a case be supposed in which the meaning of the words, if taken in their proper signification, comprehends more than the known end intended by the legislator. In this case, if it is absolutely certain that the words as used by the legislator and interpreted according to their proper signification would include more than the end intended by him, the meaning of the law must be restricted to conform to the

[44] Reg. 88, R. J., in VI°; cf. Michiels, *loc. cit.*

intended end.[45] Before such a procedure can rightfully be regarded as allowable, it is necessary that the end be *certainly* known, and that it be the *adequate* end, including not only the primary and motivating ends but even those which are secondary and incidental. For the legislator may have certain secondary reasons which justify his employment of words whose meaning would signify more than the aparent end would warrant. When, however, the complete and exclusive end of the law is known beyond doubt, but the words taken in their full proper signification have a wider meaning than is justified by the end, then and only then will the meaning of the words suffer a limitation from the end or purpose of the law.[46] Restriction, therefore, is allowed only in those very rare cases wherein the application of the words of the law to the case in question would lead to an absurdity and injustice altogether alien to the will of the legislator.[47] According to the unanimous opinion of the authors, canon 850 should receive a restrictive interpretation. The pastor has the right to bring Holy Communion to the sick as Holy Viaticum. But, lest the reception of this Sacrament be made too difficult (and thus there emerge a result that stands contrary to the intention of the legislator), this is understood of Holy Viaticum only when It is initially administered, since only on that occasion is the sick person bound to receive It (canon 464, § 1). Therefore other priests are permitted to bring Holy Viaticum to the sick person after the pastor has exercised his right. Again, though no one may validly receive an academic degree in Theology and Canon Law if he has not completed his study of scholastic philosophy,[48] nevertheless, laymen who have not studied

[45] Michiels, *ibid.*, p. 553.

[46] Suarez, *De Legibus,* Lib. VI, cap. V, nn. 3-7; Michiels, *loc. cit.*

[47] D'Annibale, *Summula Theologiae Moralis,* Pars I, *Prolegomena,* n. 187; Suarez, *De Legibus,* Lib. VI, cap. V, n. 3; Van Hove, *De Legibus Ecclesiasticis,* p. 270.

[48] Pius X, litt. encyl. *Pascendi dominici gregis,* 8 sept. 1907, (cf. *Fontes,* n. 680). Cf. n. 44, II, § 2, of the document: "Theologiae ac iuris canonici laurea nullus in posterum donetur qui statum curriculum in scholistica philosophia antea non elaboraverit. Quod si donetur, inaniter donatus esto." This is confirmed by the S. C. de Seminariis et Studiorum Universitatibus, Declaratio, 29 aprilis 1927—*AAS,* XIX (1927), 194.

philosophy may be admitted to the study of Canon Law, because the end of the law is to avert the danger which might arise for clerics and priests as ocasioned by their neglect of the study of philosophy.[49] This reason scarcely exists for laymen, who study Canon Law for the purpose of assisting in juridical matters in the Roman Curia.[50]

Article II. The Circumstances of the Law

Circumstances are accessory and extrinsic factors which accompany and surround the law.[51]

Although these are extrinsic to the will of the legislator, they affect it in some manner and have an influence on the formation of the law. Such external factors exist for every law, for a law is a psychological phenomenon intimately connected with the social phenomena that gave rise to it.[52] Circumstances can throw much light upon the mind of the legislator, and it has been said that to know the historical circumstances under which a law was made is practically the same as knowing its cause.[53] However, these may be many and diversified.

Let it be remembered that, since the law consists in only the actual will of the legislator, and since the duty of the interpreter is restricted to the disclosure and manifestation of this will, the circumstances are to be examined with the purpose of discovering how they affected the will of the legislator at the time when the law was made.[54]

Sufficient importance must be attached to an understanding of the *origin and historical evolution* of the actual law as it exists today. The law that today binds did not suddenly come into being; it is the result of the customs of the faithful, the statutes of the social authority, and the social necessities of times past. That the legislator himself attributes importance to this consider-

[49] S. C. de Seminariis et Studiorum Universitatibus, *Declaratio,* 11 aprilis 1928—*AAS,* XX (1928), 157.

[50] Van Hove, *De Legibus Ecclesiasticis,* p. 270.

[51] Abbo-Hannan, *The Sacred Canons,* I, 38.

[52] Michiels, *ibid.,* p. 531.

[53] Cicognani, *Canon Law,* p. 612.

[54] Michiels, *loc. cit.*

ation is evidenced from canon 6, in which, besides adverting to the general principle that the Code in a great measure retains the former discipline, he stresses also the practical rules for the interpretation of the laws which either completely or partially are derived from the past. Thus Michiels notes, by way of an example, that one could scarcely understand the censures contained in the Code without having recourse, in almost every instance, to the Constitution *Sedis Apostolicae* of Pius IX, issued by him on October 12, 1869,[55] which in turn could receive clarification from many articles of the Bull *In Coena Domini,* issued by Pope Urban VIII in 1627.[56]

The actual *occasion* for the making of the law may give some indication of the mind of the legislator. For example, he may desire to eradicate some abuse, to mitigate a certain discipline, or to make it more severe. However, one must be certain how these circumstances actually influenced the legislator, for sometimes a particular circumstance in a given locality may be the occasion for the enactment of a general law, and therefore it would be of little value in interpretation.[57] Only those circumstances are to be considered which incontestably served to influence the legislator. The motives may sometimes be discovered from the preparatory acts preceding the enactment of the law, or from other authentic documents.[58] Acts preparatory to the drawing up of the law are of value as a means of searching out its true sense. Though it is true that the preparation of ecclesiastical law ordinarily is not done by the legislator himself, nor by a legislative body, but rather by expert jurists,[59] who however have no legislative power, the examination of their acts will cast

55 *Fontes,* n. 552.

56 *Bullarium Romanum,* V, 125; Michiels, *ibid.,* p. 532. Cf. also Gasparri, *Tractatus Canonicus de Matrimonio* (ed. nova, 2 vols., Romae: Typis Polyglottis Vaticanis, 1932), II, 264-265, n. 1217, in order to see what light he throws on canon 1139 by reporting the deliberations of the Commission on the reply of the Holy Office of March 2, 1904.

57 Van Hove, *op. cit.,* p. 272.

58 Michiels, *ibid.,* p. 418.

59 The work of preparing the Code is well described in Cardinal Gasparri's Preface.

light on the meaning of the law, and if the legislator should use the very words proposed by these learned men it is rightly presumed that he understands them in the same way, unless the contrary is evident.[60] Again, the deliberation given by the consultors in solving doubts proposed to the Sacred Congregations often clarify the decisions and decrees issued by these Sacred Congregations. One must beware, however, lest the opinion of one or a few be taken for the common mind and intention.[61] Even the common mind and intention of the consultors does not *necessarily* represent the mind of the legislator.[62]

The *subsequent* interpretation and the common manner in which the law is observed by the subjects are also to be classified as circumstances. Though it is true that neither custom introduced by the community, nor the common opinion of authors who interpret the law, intrinsically (*per se*) and directly manifests the intention of the legislator, since these are of a later time, it cannot be denied that, ordinarily at least, they produce moral certitude that such was the mind of the legislator.[63]

Some authors combine the *recursus ad circumstantias legis* with the *mens legislatoris* into one rule of interpretation.[64] Others treat it as a separate norm.[65] Still others, perhaps in greater number, unite it with the *finis legis*.[66] This last combination seems more in conformity with the wording of the Code, which appears to unite the end and circumstances of the law into one rule of interpretation: ". . . *ad legis finem* AC *circum-*

60 Michiels, *ibid.*, pp. 532, 533; Van Hove, *op. cit.*, p. 272.

61 Van Hove, *op. cit.*, p. 273.

62 Van Hove, *loc. cit.*: ". . . lex dicit iussum superioris ecclesiastici, qui est una individua persona ordinarie loquendo, et lege manifestat suam voluntatem."—B. Ojetti, *Commentarium in Codicem Iuris Canonici* (4 vols., Romae: Apud Aedes Universitatis Gregorianae, 1927-1931), Vol. I, p. 133, note 4 (hereafter cited Ojetti).

63 Michiels, *loc. cit.* Cf. canon 29.

64 E.g., Van Hove, *op. cit.*, pp. 272-274.

65 E.g., Michiels, *ibid.*, pp. 530-533; Ojetti, I, 144, 145.

66 Cf. Cappello, *Summa Iuris Canonici,* I, 68; Vermeersch-Creusen, *Epitome Iuris Canonici,* I, 123; Schmidt, *The Principles of Authentic Interpretation in Canon 17 of the Code of Canon Law,* p. 144.

stantias est recurrendum."[67] Suarez also seemed to unite these two when treating of the *finis legis*. He observed that although the end of the law, when expressly stated in the law, offered a strong indication of the mind of the legislator, nevertheless, some doubt could still remain, and therefore other circumstances had to be taken into account.[68]

Article III. The Mind of the Legislator

Canon 18 finally directs that recourse to the mind of the legislator be used as a means of interpretation. However, since the ultimate end of all interpretation is the disclosure of the mind or intent of the legislator as it is expressed in the law,[69] it is the cause of some confusion that it should also be used as a means of interpretation. For this reason authors differ in their understanding of the *mens legislatoris*, as that term is employed in canon 18.

This much is agreed upon by all: the mind of the legislator must be *revealed* by the law. If the law does not reveal the mind and intent of the legislator there is no law, even though it is known what the legislator actually intends to say.[70] If the interpreter knows what the legislator means by the law, and yet this intention is not expressed within the words of the law, he is not allowed to supply for deficiencies nor may he completely distort the meaning of the words in order to make the law conform to the intention of the legislator, for the mind of the legislator must in some way be reflected within and expressed by the wording of the law.[71]

[67] Schmidt, *op. cit.*, p. 144.

[68] Suarez, *De Legibus*, Lib. VI, cap. I, n. 20.

[69] Suarez, *De Legibus*, Lib. VI, cap. I, n. 12; Michiels, *ibid.*, p. 544.

[70] Suarez, *De Legibus*, Lib. VI, cap. I, n. 13; Michiels, *op. cit.*, I, pp. 554, 555; Van Hove, *op. cit.*, p. 273.

[71] ". . . quia homines non possunt mentem alterius hominis percipere, nisi ex verbis ejus . . . quomodo ergo potest sensus legis, quae in verbis consistit, ex mente sumi, cum ipsa mens per verba tantum nobis potest innotescere? Et confirmatur: nam si legislator per verba legis suam mentem non declarat, non constitueretur lex, nec oriretur obligatio, etiamsi ex aliis conjecturis possemus aliquo modo voluntatem legislatoris cognoscere, quia lex non constituitur voluntate Principis nisi per verba legis sufficienter expressa, quia voluntas sola non sufficit per se ad obligandum,

According to some authors, the *mens legislatoris* in canon 18 is not really another distinct subsidiary means of interpretation, but is revealed by the other means already indicated in the canon (words, parallel passages, circumstances, and the end of the law) and rather indicates the entire scope and supreme rule of all interpretation, and it is this supreme rule that sometimes permits words (*in obscuris*) to be understood in a less proper sense.[72]

While it is true that the means or rules already given in canon 18 are all of them so many means for discovering the mind of the legislator, it seems that here the legislator intended that the *mens legislatoris* should represent still another and a distinct norm of interpretation. This opinion seems justified by the wording of the canon, which places the *mens legislatoris* side by side with the other distinct means of interpretation. It is another aid for the discovering of what is contained in the law, and for rendering its meaning certain.

In a wide sense the *mens legislatoris* seems to be the general disposition with which the legislator, in making his laws, is inspired, animated and directed; and it is his will that his laws be interpreted in accordance with this disposition.[73] Wherefore the mind of the legislator in general is:

1) That all his laws be interpreted in accordance with the dictates of right reason and justice. Injustice, absurdity and uselessness must all be shunned, even if in order to do this it is necessary sometimes to interpret words in an improper sense.[74]

2) That the universal law, the decrees of the Holy See, and also the enactments issued by subordinate legislators, in virtue of faculties conceded to them by the Holy See, must be interpreted according to the norms used in the Church's universal law and in accordance with the *stylus* and *praxis* of the Roman

---

nec enim est satis, quod aliunde privatim innotescat, sed necesse est, ut in ipsa lege sufficienter contineatur."—Suarez, *De Legibus,* Lib. VI, cap. I, n. 13. Cf. also Michiels, *op. cit.,* I, 554; Van Hove, *op. cit.,* p. 250 and p. 273.

[72] Van Hove, *op. cit.,* p. 273.

[73] U. Beste, *Introductio in Codicem* (3. ed., Collegeville, Minn.: St. John's Abbey Press, 1946), p. 18 (hereafter cited as Beste).

[74] Suarez, *De Legibus,* Lib. VI, cap. I, n. 17; Reiffenstuel, *Ius Canonicum Universum,* Lib. I, tit. II, nn. 395 and 396; Michiels, *ibid.,* p. 557; Van Hove, *loc. cit.*

Curia. The laws of subordinate legislators are to receive their interpretation in accordance with the custom and statutes of the place, from the universal law itself and the *praxis* of the Holy See.[75]

3) That laws be interpreted with canonical equity. Canonical equity here means that humanity or humaneness of the ecclesiastical superior, by which he attempts to temper the rigorous severity of the legal text in his application of the law to concrete cases. Since laws are generally brief in form and suppose ordinary contingencies, they do not always embrace situations for which some mitigation seems indicated. Equity, therefore, is a quality altogether proper to Canon Law.[76] However, it pertains more properly to interpretation and to the application of the law by the legislator or the judge to particular cases, and if it necessitates an actual changing of the meaning of the law to suit the case, it is no longer interpretation in the proper sense of the word, but rather an application of the principles of *epikeia* or equity in the strict sense.[77]

The mind of the legislator in particular is:

1) That, when the law remains obscure, recourse be had to the rules of law in cases wherein they may help to clarify the law.

[75] Michiels, *loc. cit.*

[76] Vermeersch-Creusen, *Epitome Iuris Canonici,* I, 129: ". . . et ideo iurisprudentia dicta est ars boni et aequi, quod in legibus interpretandis bonum et aequum semper intueri debet, etiam si interdum oporteat verborum rigorem temperare, ne ab aequo et bono naturali discedatur."—Suarez, *De Legibus,* Lib. V, cap. II, n. 10; "In omnibus quidem, maxime tamen in iure, aequitas spectanda est."—D. (50. 17) 90.

[77] Though most authors in treating of interpretation speak also of *epikeia,* this is really not interpretation. *Epikeia* is a benign application of the law according to what is just and good, that is, an interpretation of the mind of the legislator, who in some particular and extraordinary case is presumed to have suspended the operation of his law. Thus it differs from interpretation in two respects: first, interpretation attempts to discover the mind of the legislator as it is expressed in the law, while *epikeia* seeks the mind of the legislator as not contained in the law; secondly, the principles of interpretation are applicable to all laws, while *epikeia* applies only to particular and exceptional cases. Cf. Maroto, *Institutiones Iuris Canonici,* I, 256; Cicognani, *Canon Law,* p. 614; Van Hove, *De Legibus Ecclesiasticis,* pp. 281-304.

For example, *"Odia restringi et favores convenit ampliari"*;[78] *"Inspicimus in obscuris, quod est verisimilius, vel quod plerumque fieri consuevit"*;[79] *"In obscuris miniusum est sequendum"*;[80] *"Contra eum, qui legem dicere potuit apertius, est interpretatio facienda"*; *etc.*[81]

It is to be understood, however, that though the rules of law are useful aids in interpretation, great caution must be observed lest they be misused or abused. Even renowned canonists occasionally fail in their application of the rules of law.[82]

2) That recourse be had to the responses given by the Sacred Congregations and also to laws and decrees issued by other ecclesiastical authorities, in cases wherein they expressly or equivalently explain the mind of the legislator, in order that the law in question may be interpreted accordingly.[83]

3) That recourse be had to other canons of the Code by which the legislator reveals the manner in which he desires laws to be interpreted,[84] to the common opinion of approved authors, and to any available valid means which may be of assistance in discovering the will of the legislator.

SCHOLION

I. The primary rule of interpretation, as stated in canon 18, is that ecclesiastical laws must be understood according to the proper meaning of the words in connection with text and context. The question could be asked: is it ever necessary to apply

[78] Reg. 15, R. J., in VI°.

[79] Reg. 45, R. J., in VI°.

[80] Reg. 30, R. J., in VI°.

[81] Reg. 57, R. J., in VI°.

[82] Cf. Roelker, "An Introduction to the Rules of Law," *The Jurist*, X (1950), 271-303; and 417-436.

[83] E.g., Pont. Intr. Comm., resp. ad can. 139, § 4, die 25 april. 1922 (*AAS*, XIV [1922], 313); resp. de voce "impedimentum," ad can. 1971, § 1, 1, die 12 mart. 1929 (*AAS*, XXI [1929], 171); S. C. de Religiosis, dubium de superioribus domorum filialium, 1 febr. 1924 (*AAS*, XVI [1924], 95).

[84] E.g., cans. 19-23; cf. Abbo-Hannan, *The Sacred Canons*, I, 38; Beste, p. 83.

the secondary rules of interpretation if the law has already become clear and certain through the application of the primary rule?

Most of the authors hold the opinion that, if after the application of the primary rule the law becomes clear, then further interpretation is out of place.[85]

Michiels admits that, if the words of the law produce certitude, there is no need to apply the secondary rules, but he denies that the true sense of the law as intended by the legislator can ever be known with certitude until all the auxiliary rules are applied to the law, and that at best the words can produce but a *presumption* of the true meaning of the law.[86]

This opinion seems somewhat exaggerated. Canon 18 simply states that ecclesiastical laws must be understood according to the proper signification of the words, in connection with text and context. At the end of this clause there is a semicolon. The next clause states, *"quae si dubia et obscura manserit . . . etc."* Certainly the understanding here seems to be that ordinarily the words will convey the meaning of the law without doubt or obscurity; but, if they do not, then recourse is to be had to the other means. Nowhere in the canon is there a basis for the assumption that the words of themselves are incapable of producing certitude. Why is it not possible to be certain of the meaning of a law from its wording alone? The examination of the other means of interpretation will lead to a better understanding of the law, but will not always and of necessity make more certain what the law commands, or prohibits, or allows.

II. If, after the application of the rules contained in canon 18, the meaning of the law remains doubtful or obscure, the principle of canon 15 goes into effect: *"Leges etiam irritantes et inhabilitantes in dubio iuris non urgent."* Another solution can derive from the interposing of recourse to the competent authority for an authentic interpretation.[87]

[85] Ojetti, I, 142; Cicognani, *Canon Law,* p. 611; Beste, p. 81; Abbo-Hannan, *The Sacred Canons,* I, 37.

[86] Michiels, *Normae Generalis Iuris Canonici,* I, 516.

[87] Michiels, *ibid.,* p. 569; Abbo-Hannan, *ibid.,* p. 39.

CONCLUSIONS

I. Roman Law furnishes many of the fundamental principles of doctrinal interpretation, and the Roman Law Glossators in their comments on the *Digest* and the Justinian *Codex* clarified the rules of interpretation therein contained and applied these rules in the solution of cases.

II. These rules were further developed and more precisely adapted to Canon Law, though some of the rules used in Canon Law were merely similar to the rules employed in Roman Law, and other rules were drawn up peculiar to Canon Law.

III. Later authors such as Suarez, Barbosa, Reiffenstuel, Schmalzgrueber, and others continued to analyze the principles contained in Roman Law, Canon Law and the *Glossae,* restating them with more precise explanations and limitations.

IV. There may be a discrepancy between the words of the law and the mind of the legislator; the end of interpretation is to disclose the mind of the legislator as manifested in the law.

V. Since the legislation contained in the Code is for the most part a restatement of the older law, canon 18 must be employed in close association with canon 6. In fact it may be said that canon 6 is after a fashion contained in canon 18.

VI. If parallel texts understood in their proper signification are truly contrary, the proper signification of the words must be abandoned for a less proper sense which will obviate the contradiction, as long as the improper sense is not unreasonable, opposed to certain affirmations of the legislator, or in conflict with principles adhered to by him. Parallel laws of the Code are to be used also as a means of interpretation for laws enacted by subordinate authorities.

VII. The law is not in principle to be extended because of similarity or identity of reason, but it includes all those cases and only those which, though not comprehended under the proper signification of the words, are however objectively necessary for the adequate fulfillment of the end which was beyond doubt intended by the legislator in making the law.

VIII. Restriction of law is allowed only in those very rare cases wherein the application of the words of the law, taken in their proper sense, to the case in question would lead to an absurdity or an injustice altogether alien to the will of the legislator.

IX. The *mens legislatoris* as mentioned in canon 18 is more than a mere indication of the scope and supreme rule of all interpretation; it represents in addition a special norm of interpretation which is external to the law itself, and thus furnishes an added means for discovering the true meaning of the law.

BIBLIOGRAPHY

Sources

Codex Iuris Canonici, Pii X Pontificis Maximi iussu disgestus Benedicti Papae XV auctoritate promulgatus, ed. Petri Card. Gasparri, Civitate Vaticana: Typis Polyglottis Vaticanis, 1917; reimpressio, 1934.

Codicis Iuris Canonici Fontes, cura Emi Petri Card. Gasparri editi, 9 vols., Romae (postea Civitate Vaticana): Typis Polyglottis Vaticanis, 1923-1939. Vols. VII-IX, ed. cura et studio Emi Iustiniani Card. Serédi.

Collectio Librorum Iuris Anteiustiniani in Usum Scholarum, Krueger-Mommsen-Studemund, Vol. I, *Gaii Institutiones,* 7. ed., Berolini: apud Weidmannos, 1923.

Corpus Iuris Canonici, Editio Lipsiensis, 2 vols., Richter-Friedberg, Lipsiae, 1879-1881: Pars Prior, *Decretum Magistri Gratiani;* Pars Secunda, *Decretalium Collectiones.*

Corpus Iuris Civilis, 3 vols., Berolini: Apud Weidmannos, 1928-1929: Vol. I, ed. stereotypa quinta decima, *Institutiones,* ed. Paulus Krueger; *Digesta,* ed. Theodorus Mommsen, retractavit Paulus Krueger; Vol. II, ed. stereotypa decima, *Codex Iustinianus,* ed. Paulus Krueger; Vol. III, ed. stereotypa quinta, *Novellae,* ed. Rudolphus Schoell; opus Schoellii morte interceptum absolvit Guilelmus Kroll.

Corpus Iuris Civilis, 5 vols., Lugduni, 1553-1557.

Decretales D. Gregorii Papae IX suae integritati una cum glossis restitutae, cum privilegio Gregorii XIII, Pont. Max., et aliorum Principum. Romae, 1582.

Decretum Gratiani emendatum et notationibus illustratum una cum glossis, Gregorii XIII, Pont. Max. iussu editum, 2 vols., Romae, 1582.

Florilegium patristicum, Fasc. V, *Vincentii Lerinensis Commonitoria,* digessit, vertit, adnotavit Gerhardus Rauschen, Bonnae, 1906.

Fontes Iuris Romani Anteiustiniani in Usum Scholarum, S. Riccobono–J. Baviera–C. Ferrini, Florentiae, 1909.

Jaffé, Philippus, *Regesta Pontificum Romanorum ab condita Ecclesia ad annum post Christum natum MCXCVIII,* 2. ed., correctam et auctam auspicis Gulielmi Wattenbach, curaverunt F. Kaltenbrunner (ad annum DXC), P. Ewald (DXC-DCCCLXXXII), S. Loewenfeld (DCCCLXXXII-MCXCVIII), 2 vols. in 1, Lipsae, 1885-1888.

Liber Sextus Decretalium D. Bonfatii Papae VIII, suae integritati una cum Clementinis et Extravagantibus, earumque Glossis restitutus, cum privilegio Gregorii XIII, Pont. Max., et aliorum Principum, Romae, 1582.

Magnum Bullarium Romanum, a Beato Leone Magno (440-461) usque ad S. D. N. Benedictum XIV (1740-1758), Editio Novissima, 8 vols., Luxemburgi, 1727.

Potthast, Augustus, *Regesta Pontificum Romanorum inde ab anno post Christum natum MCXCVIII ad annum MCCCIV,* 2 vols., Berolini, 1874-1875.

REFERENCE WORKS

Abbo, John A., and Hannan, Jerome D., *The Sacred Canons,* 2 vols., St. Louis: B. Herder Book Co., 1952.

Alphonsus de Castro, *De potestate legis poenalis,* Parisiis, 1578.

Aquinas, Thomas, *Summa Theologica,* 6 vols., Taurini (Italia): Marietti, 1932.

Aristotelis, *Opera,* Lugduni, 1561.

Augustine, Charles, *A Commentary on the New Code of Canon Law,* 8 vols., Vol. I, 2. ed., St. Louis: Herder, 1916.

Baldus de Ubaldis, *In Decretalium Volumen Commentaria,* Venetiis, 1580.

Baldus de Ubaldis, *Commentaria in Digestum,* 3 vols., Venetiis, 1572.

Barbosa, Augustinus, *Tractatus Varii,* Lugduni, 1660.

Bartolus a Saxoferrato, *Omnia quae extant Opera,* 10 vols., Sexta Editio, Venetiis, 1590-1615.

Beste, Udalricus, *Introductio in Codicem,* Editio Tertia, Collegeville, Minn.: St. John's Abbey Press, 1946.

Blat, Albertus, *Commentarium Textus Codicis Canonici,* 6 vols., Vol. I, Romae: Ex Typographia Pontificia in Instituto Pii IX, 1921.

Bouscaren, T. Lincoln, and Ellis, Adam C., *Canon Law,* Milwaukee: The Bruce Publishing Company, 1946.

Buckland, W. W., *A Text-Book of Roman Law From Augustus to Justinian,* 2. ed., Cambridge University Press, 1932.

Cappello, Felix M., *Summa Iuris Canonici,* 3 vols., Romae: Apud Aedes Universitatis Gregorianae, Vols. I-II, 4. ed., 1945; Vol. III, ed. altera, 1940.

Catholic Encyclopedia, The: An International Work of Reference on the Constitution, Doctrine, Discipline and History of the Catholic Church, edited by Charles J. Herbermann, Edward A. Pace, Conde B. Pallen, Thomas J. Shahan, John J. Wynne, assisted by numerous collaborators, 15 vols., Index and Supplement, New York, 1907-1922.

Cicero, M. Tullius, *Scripta Quae Manserunt Omnia,* 5 vols., C. F. W. Mueller, Gulielmus Friedrich, Lipsiae: B. G. Teubner, 1893-1905.

Cicognani, Amleto, *Canon Law,* 2. ed., Reprint, Westminster, Maryland: The Newman Press, 1949.

Conte a, Coronata, Matthaeus, *Institutiones Iuris Canonici,* 5 vols., Vol. I, II, 2. ed. Taurini: Ex Officina Marietti, 1939.

Cuq, Edouard, *Manuel des Institutions Jurisdiques des Romains,* 2 vols., Paris, 1891-1902.

Cyclopedic Law Dictionary, The, Walter A. Shumaker and George Foster Longsdorf, 2. ed., by James Cahill, Chicago: Callagahan and Company, 1922.

D'Annibale, Iosephus, *Summula Theologiae Moralis*, Pars I, *Prolegomena*, 5. ed., Romae, 1908.

Dictionnaire de Droit Canonique, Paris: Letouzey et Ané, 1924-

Fagnanus, Prosper, *Commentaria Super Quinque Libros Decretalium*, 5 vols., Romae, 1661.

Gasparri, Petrus Card., *Tractatus Canonicus de Matrimonio*, editio nova, 2 vols., Romae: Typis Polyglottis Vaticanus, 1932.

Gaii Institutionum Commentarii Quattuor, 6. ed. B. Kuebler, Lipsiae: in Aedibus B. G. Teubneri, 1928.

Geny, François, *Méthode d'Interpretation et Sources en Droit Privé Positif*, 2. ed., 2 vols., Paris: Librairie Generale de Droit et de Jurisprudence, 1932.

Guilfoyle, Merlin J., *Custom*, The Catholic University of America Canon Law Studies, n. 105, Washington, D. C.: The Catholic University of America, 1937.

Hostiensis (Henricus de Segusio), *In Decretalium Commentaria*, 3 vols., Venetiis, 1581.

Ioannes Andreae, *In VI Libros Decretalium Novella Commentaria*, 5 vols., 1581.

Jolowicz, H. F., *Historical Introduction to the Study of Roman Law*, London: Cambridge University Press, 1932.

Krueger, Paul, *Histoire des Sources du Droit Romain*, Manuel des Antiquites Romaines, Mommsen–Marquardt–Krueger, Paris, 1894.

Lee, Robert Warden, *The Elements of Roman Law with a Translation of the Institutes of Justinian*, London: Sweet and Maxwell Limited, 1944.

Lega, Michael, *Praelectiones in Textum Iuris Canonici, De Iudiciis Ecclesiasticis*, 4 vols., Lib. I, Vol. I, 1896; Lib. I, Vol. II, 1898; Lib. II, Vol. III, 1899; Lib. II, Vol. IV, 1901, Romae.

Maroto, Philippus, *Institutiones Iuris Canonici ad Normam Novi Codicis*, Vol. I, 3. ed., Romae: apud Commentarium pro Religiosis, 1921.

Merkelbach, B. H., *Summa Theologiae Moralis* (2, ed., 3 vols., Parisiis: Typis Desclée, De Brouwer et Soc., 1935-1936).

Michiels, Gommarus, *Normae Generales Iuris Canonici*, editio altera, 2 vols., Typis Societatis S. Joannis Evangelistae, Desclée et Socii, Parisiis-Tornaci-Romae, 1949.

Migne, P. J., *Patrologiae Cursus Completus*—Series Latina, 221 vols., Parisiis, 1844-1855.

Mitteis, L.–Levy, H.–Rabel, E., *Index Interpollationum Quae in Iustiniani Digestis inesse dicuntur*, 3 vols., Weimar: Hermann Böhlaus Nachfolger, 1929-1935.

Neuberger, Nicholas J., *Canon 6, or the Relation of the Codex Iuris Canonici to Preceding Legislation*, The Catholic University of America Canon Law Studies, n. 44, Washington: The Catholic University of America, 1927.

Noval, Josephus P., *Codificationis Iuris Canonici Recensio Historico-Apologetica et Codicis Piano-Benedictini Notitia Generalis* (Romae, 1918).

Ojetti, Benedictus, *Commentarium in Codicem Iuris Canonici,* 4 vols., Romae: Apud Aedes Universitatis Gregorianae, 1927-1931.

Ottaviani, Alaphridus, *Institutiones Iuris Publici Ecclesiastici,* 2. ed., 2 vols., Civitate Vaticana: Typis Polyglottis Vaticanis, 1935-1936.

Panormitanus, Abbas (Nicolaus de Tudeschis), *Omnia Quae Extant Commentaria in Decretales,* 6 vols., Venetiis, 1588.

Pirhing, Ernricus, *Ius Canonicum in V Libros Decretalium,* 4 vols., Dilingae, 1722.

Regatillo, E., *Institutiones Iuris Canonici,* 2 vols., Santander: Sal Terrae, 1941-1942.

Reiffenstuel, Anacletus, *Ius Canonicum Universum,* ed. novissima, 5 vols., Romae, 1831-1834.

Roncaglia, C., *Moralis Theologia Universa,* 3 vols., Venetiis, 1760.

Salmanticenses, *Cursus Theologiae Moralis,* 6 vols. in 4, Venetiis, 1714-1728.

Saltet, Louis, *Les Réordinations: Étude sur le Sacrement de l'Ordre,* 2. ed., Paris, 1907.

Savigny, F. C., *Sistema del diritto romano attuale,* Vol. I, Traduzione dall'originale tedesco di Vittorio Scialoja, Torino, 1886.

Schmalzgrueber, Franciscus, *Ius Ecclesiasticum Universum,* 12 vols., Romae, 1843-1845.

Schmidt, John Rogg, *The Principles of Authentic Interpretation in Canon 17 of the Code of Canon Law,* The Catholic University of America Canon Law Studies, n. 141, Washington, D. C.: The Catholic University of America Press, 1941.

Sherman, Charles F., *Roman Law in the Modern World,* 2. ed., 3 vols., New York: Baker, Voorhis, & Co., 1924.

Sohm, R., *The Institutes, A Textbook of the History and System of Roman Private Law,* 3. ed., translated by J. C. Ledlie, Oxford: Clarendon Press, 1926.

Suarez, Franciscus, *Opera Omnia,* 28 vols., ed. L. Vivès, Parisiis, 1856-1861, Vols. V-VI, *Tractatus de Legibus et Legislatore Deo.*

Toso, Albertus, *Ad Codicem Juris Canonici Commentaria Minora,* Vols. I-II, Romae et Taurini: P. Marietti, 1920-1922.

Tuschus, Dominicus, *Practicae Conclusiones Iuris in Omni Foro Frequentiores,* 8 vols., Lugduni, 1634; Additiones, Vol. IX, Lugduni, 1670.

Van Hove, A., *Commentarium Lovaniense in Codicem Iuris Canonici,* Vol. I, *Prolegomena,* 2. ed., Mechliniae: H. Dessain, 1945; Vol. II, *De Legibus Ecclesiasticis,* Mechiniae: H. Dessain, 1930.

Vermeersch, A.-Creusen, J., *Epitome Iuris Canonici,* 3 vols., Mechliniae-Romae: Dessain. Vol. I, 7. ed., 1949; Vol. II, 6. ed., 1940; Vol. III, 6. ed., 1946.

Waldron, Joseph Francis, *The Minister of Baptism,* The Catholic University of America Canon Law Studies, n. 170, Washington, D. C.: The Catholic University of America Press, 1942.

Wermz, Franciscus X., *Ius Decretalium,* 6 vols., Romae, 1898-1914.

Woywod, Stanislaus, *A Practical Commentary on the Code of Canon Law,* revised by Calistus Smith, revised and enlarged edition, 2 vols., New York: Jos. F. Wagner, Inc., 1948.

Zallinger, Jac. Ant., *Institutionum Iuris Ecclesiastici Publici et Privati Liber Subsidiarius I,* Romae, 1823.

Articles

Brems, A., "De Interpretatione Authentica Codicis I.C. per Pont. Commisionem," *Jus Pontificium,* XV (1935), 161-190; 298-313; XVI (1936), 78-105; 217-256.

Le Bras, Gabriel, "La Doctrine, source des collectiones canoniques," *Recueil d'Etudes sur les Sources du Droit en l'Honneur de François Geny* (3 vols., Paris: Recueil Sirey, 1934), I, 69-76.

Roelker, Edward, "An Introduction to the Rules of Law," *The Jurist,* X (1950), 271-303; 417-436.

Schiller, A. Arthur, "Roman Interpretatio and Anglo-American Interpretation and Construction," *Virginia Law Review,* XXVII (1940-1941), 733-768.

Periodicals

Jus Pontificium, Romae, 1921-1940.

Jurist, The, Washington, D. C., 1941-

Virginia Law Review, The, The Virginia Law Review Association, University, Virginia, 1913-

ABBREVIATIONS

AAS—*Acta Apostolicae Sedis*
Commonitoria—*Florilegium Patristicum,* Fasc. V: *Vincentii Lerinensis Commonitoria* (digessit, vertit, adnotavit Gerhardus Rauschen, Bonnae, 1906)
Cod. Com.—*Commisio ad Codicis Canones authentice Interpretandos*
Fontes—*Codidis Iuris Canonici Fontes*
MPL—Migne, *Patrologia, Series Latina*

ALPHABETICAL INDEX

BIOGRAPHICAL NOTE

Matthew Shekleton was born on November 29, 1915, in Lawler, Iowa. He received his primary education in Our Lady of Mount Carmel School there, and then attended Mater Dolorosa Preparatory Seminary in Hillside, Illinois. In September of 1933 he entered the Servite Novitiate in Granville, Wisconsin, where he made his simple profession in September of the following year. His philosophical and theological studies he pursued at Mount St. Philip Monastery in Milwaukee, Wisconsin, and at the Servite International College of St. Alexis in Rome, where he was ordained to the priesthood on November 5, 1939. After having served as a teacher in St. Philip High School in Chicago, Mater Dolorosa Seminary, and Stonebridge Priory in Lake Bluff, Illinois, he enrolled in the School of Canon Law at the Catholic University of America, in 1950. He received the Baccalaurate degree in Canon Law in June, 1951, and the Licentiate degree in Canon Law in June, 1952.

CANON LAW STUDIES *

337. Bourque, Rev. John R., S.T.L., J.C.L., The Judicial Power of the Church—Canon 1553, § 1.
338. Cornell, Rev. Charles E., A.B., S.T.B., J.C.L., The Juridical Status of Heretics and Schismatics in Good Faith.
339. Fitzgerald, Rev. William Francis, A.B., S.T.L., J.C.L., The Parish Census and the *Liber Status Animarum*.
340. Kubik, Rev. Stanislaus J., S.T.D., J.C.L., Invalidity of Dispensations According to Canon 84, § 1.
341. Nugent, Rev. John Gerard, C.M., J.C.L., Ordination in Societies of the Common Life.
342. Peterson, Rev. Casimir Melvyn, S.S., A.B., S.T.L., J.C.L., Spiritual Care in Diocesan Seminaries.
343. Reiss, Rev. John Charles, A.B., S.T.L., J.C.L., The Time and Place of Sacred Ordination.
344. Sheehan, Rev. Joseph George, J.C.L., The Obligation of Respect and Obedience of Clerics to Their Ordinary—Canon 127.
345. Shekleton, Rev. Matthew M., O.S.M., J.C.L., Doctrinal Interpretation of Law.
346. Viau, Rev. Roger, S.T.L., J.C.L., Doubt in Canon Law.
347. Walsh, Rev. Donnell Anthony, A.B., J.C.L., The New Law on Secular Institutes.

* For a complete list of the available numbers of this series apply to the Catholic University of America Press, 620 Michigan Avenue, N.E., Washington (17), D.C.

www.ingramcontent.com/pod-product-compliance
Lightning Source LLC
LaVergne TN
LVHW050204080826
844660LV00012B/347
* 9 7 8 0 8 1 3 2 2 5 1 3 5 *